BENCHMARKS XXIV

The Life and Legacy of JOSEPH L. TAURO
24th United States District Judge
for the District of Massachusetts

Richard d'A. Belin

MCLE
LEGAL
HERITAGE
Series

ISBN: 1-57589-685-0

LCCN: 2011939142

Massachusetts Continuing Legal Education, Inc.
Ten Winter Place, Boston, MA 02108-4751
800-966-6253 | Fax 617-482-9498 | www.mcle.org

FOREWORD

THE UNITED STATES DISTRICT COURT for the District of Massachusetts was among the initial courts created by the First Federal Congress in the Judiciary Act of 1789. As the Court slipped into its third century, a sense began to crystallize that its institutional history was sliding away. The last of the judges appointed before World War II, Charles Edward Wyzanski, Jr., had died in 1986. Judge Wyzanski, the fifteenth judge, had himself appeared before or served with all but the first seven of the judges. His encyclopedic recollections and forceful insights could no longer be tapped. Plainly, a meaningful way had to be found to ensure that the percipient perspectives of other long-serving judges, and those of their generations, could be preserved to ensure that avenues of access to the court's history would not be lost.

A special bicentennial issue of the *Massachusetts Law Review*, commemorating the Massachusetts federal courts, was published in 1989. Through a diverse set of articles on multiple topics from the history of the federal courts in Massachusetts, that issue disclosed some of the richness of the District Court's history. In 1994, an overview of the court's history was published in the Annual Report of the Massachusetts Supreme Judicial Court Historical Society. Yet the sense remained that a means needed to be found to capture and convey more deeply the vitality and nuance of the Court's history. The traditional vehicles for that conveyance, the potted institutional history or the transcripts of oral histories, seemed alternatively wooden and formulaic or destined for inaccessible oblivion. An insight provided by a son of Massachusetts, Ralph Waldo Emerson, pointed in a fruitful direction. "[T]here is properly no history," Emerson observed, "only biography."

Fortunately, the bar of the Court has among its members, Richard d'A. Belin, an experienced and distinguished former litigator, who recently retired to pursue the writing of biographies. Belin, who had also served as a law clerk to the late David S. Nelson—the twenty-eighth judge of the Court—was the ideal person to initiate a program of judicial biography that would make institutional history come alive and make oral history accessible, through a series of life stories of the judges of the Court. These would be told in large part through the voices of the judges themselves, those who have appeared before them, their colleagues and others who have known them well.

It is this program's further good fortune that the first subject of the Court's judicial biography initiative, the senior-most judge of the Court in point of service, Joseph L. Tauro, has lived a vivid life of great drama in the public realm of Massachusetts, including for the past thirty-nine years as the Commonwealth's twenty-fourth United States District Judge. The initial fruits of the Court's judicial biography project consequently tell the story of the Court from the perspective of the first judge to graduate from college after World War II and take that story into the first two decades of the twenty-first century.

The intent of the program is to continue with such biographies, beginning with the longest-serving judges. Belin is now at work on a biography of Rya W. Zobel, the court's twenty-ninth—and its first female—judge. His biography of Judge Tauro sets a formidable benchmark in making human the court as an institution. With support from the Attorney Admissions Fund of the United States District Court and the resources of MCLE, which has undertaken publication through its Legal Heritage series, the rich history of the Commonwealth's federal trial court is becoming available to members of the bar and to the public at large through a tapestry woven from the threads of the lives of individual judges. As additional biographies are added, it is our expectation that, in the words of Justice Holmes, by "weaving...figures of the ever-lengthening past," they will disclose more fully "to the discerning eye" the progress of the law in the United States District Court for the District of Massachusetts.

DOUGLAS P. WOODLOCK
August 2011

ABOUT JUDGE TAURO

JOSEPH L. TAURO'S LONG CAREER as a federal judge took what would turn out to be its most fateful turn in its first year. In May of 1973, just five months into his tenure, Tauro took a tour of the Belchertown State School, a Massachusetts state institution for the intellectually disabled, which was the subject of a lawsuit pending before him. Shocked by what he saw, Tauro told the state's lawyer that there would be no trial. Instead, the state was told to negotiate a consent decree specifying what would be done and to begin immediately the extensive process of remaking the institution.

Similar suits soon were filed regarding four other state institutions for the intellectually disabled, and each was assigned to Judge Tauro. Now, more than thirty-five years later, after numerous tours of facilities, scores of court hearings, periods of cooperation, and periods of confrontation, the resulting transformation has been extraordinary. Massachusetts' care of the intellectually disabled is among the best in the country.

Another major institutional reform case, the *Rogers* case, went to trial before Tauro a few years after that first tour of Belchertown. Tauro's ruling in the *Rogers* case banned the use of solitary confinement and forced medication on patients in state psychiatric institutions, except in emergency situations. The ruling, and the resulting *"Rogers* orders," required as a precondition to forced medication, became and continue to be the prevailing standard in Massachusetts and many other states.

Judge Tauro also presided over and decided two important cases raising issues of race: a challenge by black voters to Boston's at-large voting system in the mid-1990s, and a challenge by white plaintiffs to the admissions system at prestigious Boston Latin Academy in the late 1990s.

In the political arena, Tauro twice drew cases involving challenges by disaffected Congressmen to the war-making powers of the President: the first over bombing in Cambodia, and the second over the war in Iraq. He has authored precedent-setting First Amendment opinions and has presided over public corruption trials and organized crime cases. He has ruled on two of the legal cases brought by opponents of the Nantucket Sound wind farm project.

Beyond the state institution cases, Tauro has also brokered or helped to broker settlements in numerous cases ranging from a high-profile, class-action suit brought by the NAACP against the Boston Housing Authority, to personal injury cases brought by individual plaintiffs.

In 2010, at a time when Tauro might have been—but was not—contemplating retirement, he again found himself in the thick of things, this time as the presiding judge in challenges brought by the Commonwealth of Massachusetts and individual plaintiffs to the Federal Defense of Marriage Act. Tauro's opinions in these gay marriage cases, issued in July 2010, were the most widely noted of his career.

Throughout it all, Judge Tauro has remained shrewd, decisive, and not afraid of controversy. This is the story of Joe Tauro's career, as told by Judge Tauro, some of his colleagues, and many who have appeared before him.

PREFACE

A THEME RUNS THROUGH THE decades of Judge Joseph Tauro's career, and it is one of social justice. Spanning the length and breadth of his public service on the federal bench, examples of the unique Tauro brand of social justice are many. He set a national precedent for the transformation of state institutions for the intellectually disabled. He called for an end to solitary confinement and forced medication of mental health patients in state psychiatric institutions. The concept of the "*Rogers* order," which bears his signature, has protected generations of individuals from unwarranted mental health treatment. Judge Tauro brought about justice in Massachusetts' public housing when he encouraged a multi-million dollar settlement ensuring that the Boston Housing Authority afford persons of color equitable treatment when seeking public housing.

A professional life of the caliber of Judge Tauro's, a career devoted to effecting social justice, is eminently instructive. By his example, lawyers may learn what it means to incorporate social justice into their life's work—such as through pro bono representation of disadvantaged clients. For this reason, Massachusetts Continuing Legal Education, Inc. (MCLE | New England) is honored to make this biography of Judge Tauro available to the Massachusetts legal community as part of the Legal Heritage publishing initiative.

ACKNLOWLEDGEMENTS

FIRST AND FOREMOST, OUR THANKS go to Hon. Joseph L. Tauro for generously permitting MCLE to publish these reflections on his personal and professional life and achievements. This book is one in a series of publications on the lives and legacies of federal judges in the District of Massachusetts. It is a worthy project of the United States District Court, overseen by Hon. Douglas P. Woodlock. MCLE thanks Judge Woodlock for his kind assistance on this project. Our thanks go also to Judge Tauro's biographer, Richard d'A. Belin of Cambridge, for his skilled authorship of this biographical work. The many photographic images in this book have been culled from Judge Tauro's personal collection as well as from several news media sources, and Mr. Belin's diligent research efforts both in gathering them and obtaining reprint permissions for them are much appreciated. Our thanks go to MCLE's Board of Trustees for its enthusiasm for this publishing project, as well as to the many members of MCLE's staff who shared their publishing expertise in the preparation of these pages.

JOHN M. (JACK) REILLY, ESQ.
Publisher
September 2011

ABOUT THE BIOGRAPHER

RICHARD D'A. BELIN recently retired from the practice of law to pursue the writing of biographies. In addition to his work for private clients, Mr. Belin is currently working on the second book in the initiative by the U.S. District Court for the District of Massachusetts to document its history through the words of its judges—a biography of Judge Rya Zobel. During his distinguished 23-year career as a civil litigator with Foley Hoag LLP, Mr. Belin tried, brought to arbitration, or settled cases in a wide variety of fields, including serving as trial counsel for the plaintiffs in the Voting Rights case that successfully challenged the redistricting of the Massachusetts House of Representatives following the census of 2000. Prior to joining Foley Hoag, Mr. Belin was law clerk to the Honorable David S. Nelson of the U.S. District Court for the District of Massachusetts and taught in public schools for five years before entering law school. He is a graduate of Yale University (B.A.), Vanderbilt University (M.A.T.), and Boston University School of Law (J.D.).

CONTENTS

CHAPTER I

Growing Up: A Wartime and Depression Kid

The Tauro family were Italian immigrants who wasted little time in taking advantage of the opportunities America offered. Joe Tauro's paternal grandparents, Orazio and his wife Emma, came to America in 1902 from the small Italian town of Bussi, in Abruzzi province, settling in a mixed-race neighborhood in Lynn, Massachusetts. They were poor and never spoke more than broken English, but Orazio was determined that his children's lives would be very different from his own.

> *Joe Tauro:* Despite my grandfather's lack of formal education, he appreciated that study and education were the only way his children would amount to anything, and he rammed that lesson home. He was a strict disciplinarian, especially when it came to his children's studies. Every night after the dinner dishes were cleared, the children sat at the kitchen table under my grandfather's watchful eye, as he drank his wine and smoked his pipe. No one moved and no one talked.

Orazio's regime succeeded remarkably. Two of his sons, Arthur and Antonio, graduated from college and went on to Boston University School of Medicine and from there to successful careers as doctors. Another son, Goliardo Joseph Tauro, Joe Tauro's father, graduated from Boston University School of Law. G. Joseph Tauro, as the father was known, went on to a career as a lawyer and later as a judge, culminating in his tenure as Chief Justice of Massachusetts' highest court, the Supreme Judicial Court.

G. Joseph married Helen Petrossi, and they bought a house in Malden at 494 Highland Avenue, just down the street from the house at 456 Highland Avenue where Orazio and Emma were living with Doctor Arthur and Arthur's wife Dorothy. When his only child, Joseph L. Tauro, was born in 1931, G. Joseph was a rising attorney. Young Joe Tauro grew up in Malden for the first fourteen years of his life.

G. Joseph Tauro, Joe Tauro's father

COURTESY OF HON. JOSEPH L. TAURO

> *Joe Tauro:* Malden was and still is a nice, middle-class city. I had an enjoyable childhood there, but as an only child I was alone a lot. I learned to play by myself. I'd hit rocks off the garage for a single, double, or whatever, depending on where it hit. I also read a lot. I loved to read, and I'm still a reader.

G. Joseph was successful enough financially so that the family came through the Depression fairly well. The war would leave more of a mark.

> *Joe Tauro:* I was never conscious of the Depression. My dad worked very hard and was successful. He gave us a happy life, and I thought we were rich, although we were far from it during those Malden days.
>
> It was the war that had a greater impact. I remember the nightly air raid alerts. My dad was an air raid warden. Our windows were blacked out and many things, such as fuel and gasoline, were hard to get. But we got along just fine, as did our neighbors. There was a great patriotic spirit, and we felt we were all in it together. That changed a bit when Italy made the big mistake of joining the war on the side of Germany and Japan, against the United States. Then it became tough to be an Italian kid living in Malden. There was a lot of name calling— "dago," "wop," "guinea," and some fights. I didn't like any of it and that may be why I am so sensitive today with respect to bigotry of any sort against anyone.

In the first half of 1945, as the Allies fought their way across Europe and retook a series of Pacific islands, Joe Tauro spent a good part of his eighth grade year in bed, rather than at Beebe Junior High in Malden.

> *Joe Tauro:* I was laid up in bed for almost six months with something that was either rheumatic fever or pneumonia. Because my uncles were doctors I got great care. I remember there was some discussion of perhaps treating me with penicillin, which was brand new and considered a wonder drug. In the end they decided not to use it because they didn't want to "waste" it on something that was not considered life threatening. They thought then that maybe you could only use it once so they were going to save it for something really serious.

Tauro got tutoring at home and managed to complete that school year.

CHAPTER 2

The Move to Swampscott and Joe's Education

As World War II ended, the Tauro family moved to a new home in Swampscott, a lovely house just a two-minute walk from the beach, which Joe thought was a mansion. But his parents decided to send him to boarding school at St. John's Prep in Danvers, Massachusetts. Things did not go very well there.

> *Joe Tauro:* I'd had no activity for months and I was fat. I couldn't play sports. They made me take it easy because they didn't know if there was any permanent damage to my heart, although they kept testing as best they could in those days. The brothers were nice to me but they were very strict. Every night it seemed like it was freezing there. I was just plain lonely, and probably too young to board.
>
> Eventually things got a bit better. They had started me in tenth grade, but then they pushed me back from the sophomore grade to the ninth grade, so I was dealing with kids more my own age, and that was a much more comfortable feeling.
>
> By spring I was able to play sports, so I went out for the ninth grade baseball team, the Eaglets, and I made it. That kind of thing made it more fun, and I went back for my sophomore year and made the varsity, but playing baseball wasn't enough and I just wasn't happy there.

Tauro transferred to another parochial school, St. Mary's in Lynn, for his junior year. It was a better fit, but still not a big success academically.

> *Joe Tauro:* I was a marginal student. I wasn't intellectually excited about school until my senior year in high school. I must have done my work because I don't recall being punished by my father for not doing it, but I didn't have any interest in it and didn't do particularly well. Once when I was either a sophomore or junior in high school, the smash hit musical "South Pacific" came out and my father bought tickets for himself, my mother, and me. I never got there, however. My report card came out, and my father got so angry about it that he gave my ticket to somebody else. He told me that I ought to be ashamed of myself. Given my great love for show business and for music, that was tough punishment.

The highlight of the year for Joe Tauro at St. Mary's was, as always, the baseball season. He played on St. Mary's varsity team for coach Pip Kennedy, who had played and managed in the minor leagues. St. Mary's was a big school, and making the varsity was not easy.

> *Joe Tauro:* At St. Mary's there were 14 kids trying out for first base and in those days I was a first baseman. The ideal first baseman is a lefty and he's tall; I'm short and right-handed. There were all these rangy kids and this one little pipsqueak. Kids would have to take turns taking throws at first. Then one day we were having an intra-squad game, and I was on first when someone hit a foul pop-up. The ball was going out of play, but it was a big, open field and I kept running after it as fast as I could. Everybody was screaming: "No play, no play," but I just kept running and at the last minute I reached out and grabbed it, with my back to the plate. I turned around and yelled "Hah!" I knew then that I had won the job because I knew what kind of guy Coach Kennedy was, and he had seen me chase that ball like I was a junkhouse dog. Was that important to me as a lesson? It's more than 60 years later and I'm still telling that story.
>
> We were never rich enough to have a crest or anything like that, but if there were a Tauro family slogan it would be "Never quit, ever." That's what my father drilled into me. He sent me a clipping once, which said that the difference between the champion horse and the horse who finishes

> second is in the last five seconds of a race. It's the horse that doesn't quit that wins.

There were other lessons learned on the baseball field too, not always through a glorious running catch.

> *Joe Tauro:* I was playing for St. Mary's. I struck out, and I came back to the bench muttering out loud about the pitcher: "That guy's lousy. He's got nothing." Pip Kennedy chastised me in front of the team, saying: "That's what you say about him after you hit a home run, not after he strikes you out."

Swampscott High School—A Turning Point

Baseball was also Joe Tauro's way into Swampscott, his new home town. Tauro got a summer job (to which he returned each year from high school through college) coaching baseball for the Swampscott Parks Department. It was a great opportunity to meet people, including other kids his own age, as well as the Swampscott High School baseball coach, Keith Jordan.

> *Joe Tauro:* I was responsible for coaching the Swampscott town team, which was made up of high school kids. We played other towns. I enjoyed that very much and later came very close to deciding to become a coach.

Tauro soon found himself switching schools again, enrolling at Swampscott High in the fall of 1948 for his senior year. It would prove to be a turning point, as things quickly began to go his way.

> *Joe Tauro:* In the fall, each of the homerooms elected a representative to the student council. A guy in my homeroom, Donnie Richards, put my name on the board to nominate me. I erased it. We did this once or twice more. Donnie was a funny guy. He pretended to be irate and told the teacher that I was erasing my name and he didn't think I had any right to do that and I ought to be sent down to the principal's office. The

> teacher told me to stop erasing my name and damned if I didn't get elected.
>
> I went to a meeting for the student council representatives for all of the homerooms. There were 13 or 14 of us sitting around the room. The question came up: who would be student council president? Norma Palleschi, who was a good friend of mine, nominated me. Everybody said that was a great idea, and I was unanimously elected, thanks to Norma's nominating me. Later I had to introduce myself to the principal, Mr. Dunn, when he was introducing me to the class.

Tauro's surprise election changed his whole attitude toward school.

> *Joe Tauro:* It was a great break for me, because it put me in a different light. You started to realize that you had some responsibility. It had a positive effect on my studies and everything else.

Another thing that had a positive effect on Tauro's studies at Swampscott High was his dad, who taking a leaf out of his father's book kept an eye on things.

> *Joe Tauro:* In Swampscott, it was a very popular thing for the kids to meet down at the library at night. They'd say goodbye to their parents and say that they were going to the library to study. I tried that the first day I went to Swampscott High, but my father said no, there wasn't going to be any of that. If I needed a book I was to tell him and he would get it for me and I would read it at home, but I could forget about nights at the Swampscott Library. My father was very shrewd and he kept me on the straight and narrow path.

Things continued to go Tauro's way when the school play, *I Remember Mama,* was cast. Tauro landed the male lead, Uncle Chris. Tauro had a serious show business itch, something he probably caught from his favorite cousins, Guy and Tony Pastor Jr., both professional singers and actors, whose dad, Tony Pastor, was a prominent band leader.

> *Joe Tauro:* Mama was a critically acclaimed human comedy. The part of Chris was a pivotal role to the plot, with many

> great comedic lines. The audience was very attentive. Their responsiveness was like music to my ears. Clearly, the show biz bug took a big bite out of me.

Despite newfound academic success and a growing interest in the theater, the highlight of the year was baseball season. Coach Keith Jordan had a fine team that year (1948–49). Joe, who had moved over a spot in the infield, was the starting second baseman. The team began chalking up wins. One win came on a really hot day.

> *Joe Tauro:* We had a tough game. I had sweat so much that they had to give me a new hat during the game because mine had become almost like paper from the sweat. I came home, drained, went up and took a shower and came back downstairs. My father said to me: "Would you like me to make spaghetti with oil?" He used to make this pasta with sardines and olive oil, which was out of this world. I was starving. Then he said: "Would you like a beer?" which was something he never offered me. He was trying to get my fluids going. I said yes. He told me I could have the beer on the condition that I stay home that night and not drive. I had to call my girlfriend, Lois Moran, to tell her that my father was going to give me a beer so I couldn't pick her up. My father did give me a beer, and I am still talking about that wonderful dinner. It was one of the best dinners I ever had in my life. That was how simple life was in those days.

The 1949 Swampscott High team lost only one game all year. When the wins kept coming in the state tournament, they found themselves in the championship game, played at storied Fenway Park. The night before the game, Tauro and many of the team members had been at the senior prom. He had gone, against his father's advice that he should stay home and go to bed early. As he danced that night with his girlfriend, Lois Moran, in the high school gym he helped to decorate, Joe Tauro thought: Life doesn't get any better than this.

The next day at Fenway Park, it looked like the old man had been right. Things went badly for Swampscott from the start.

Tauro at bat in the championship game at Fenway Park

COURTESY OF HON. JOSEPH L. TAURO

> *Joe Tauro:* For most of the game we played lousy. Then in the eighth inning we finally caught fire, and in the ninth we went on to win the game. I scored the tying run. I came home, expecting a big hug from my father. Instead he was very cool to me. "I hope you learned your lesson," he said. It turned out that when we fell way behind he had left the game early and didn't realize we had come back to win it. He was so embarrassed that he had quit on us that he treated the team to a wonderful banquet at Swampscott's best restaurant.
>
> It was a thrill to play in Fenway. The left wall is pretty close, but to me it seemed like it was 400 miles away. If I was on third base I couldn't hit it out!

Tauro Sr. had ignored his own advice to never quit, but the team finished with a 17-1 record and Swampscott's only state baseball championship. Joe Tauro was an All-State honorable mention at second base. It was a great season, which team members and Coach Jordan continue to celebrate at reunions. In December 2010, the team was elected to the Town of Swampscott Hall of Fame.

> *Joe Tauro:* We just had our 60th reunion a short time ago at a little restaurant in Swampscott. Coach Jordan came. He stands up straight as an arrow and has a handshake that could break your arm, and he's in his late nineties. We had a lot of people return, including all of the first team infield: Freddy Carone at

> first, me at second, Alex Kurpis at short and Patsy Tratola at third. Freddy Carone said: "That's how we won the state championship three Italians and a Greek."

Swampscott High state champion baseball team: Patsy Tratola is in the bottom row 4th from left, Alex Kurpis to his right, then Joe Tauro. Fred Carone is back row 4th from right. Coach Jordan is back right.

COURTESY OF HON. JOSEPH L. TAURO

One cloudy experience from those otherwise happy Swampscott High School years remains in Tauro's memory. During the spring of his senior year, a classmate and friend, Dick Coan, told him that the Tedesco Country Club in Swampscott was offering a special summer golf membership for high school kids at the bargain rate of $90. He urged Tauro to apply and he did.

A few weeks later Tauro's father spoke with him and asked if he had applied to the Tedesco Country Club. Tauro told him he had.

> *Joe Tauro:* My father said to me: "Don't you know that Tedesco doesn't have Italian members?" I said I did not. I still recall the rather empty feeling I had realizing that there was that kind of prejudice. Up to that point, I had never experienced any sort of ethnic or religious prejudice, other than name calling during the Second World War.

Tauro's father went on to tell his son that the president of Tedesco had called and told him about the application. He said that having an Italian member of Tedesco was long overdue, but that Tedesco wanted Tauro's father to submit a family application rather than rely on the student application. Tauro Sr. said he thanked the Tedesco president for the offer, but declined, saying: "I am not going to be any Jackie Robinson," a reference to the pioneering black major league baseball player.

> *Joe Tauro:* That all happened about 60 years ago, and I have been to the Tedesco Club many times since then. But I have to say that any time I go there, or even drive by, the memory of that student application comes back to me.

Brown University

In the fall of 1949, Tauro began his freshman year at Brown University. Based on his first three years of high school, Brown would have been out of Tauro's reach, but senior year at Swampscott High had changed all that. When it came time for college applications, Brown was his first choice.

> *Joe Tauro:* There was a kid by the name of Mike Stein, who was a good Swampscott athlete. He went to Brown and played football there. Mike had a summer job down by Fisherman's Beach in Swampscott, which in those days was a very pretty beach. He worked in a parking lot there. He was a very gregarious guy, always talking about Brown. He said he worked hard all summer so when he went back to college he could go as a gentleman. No waiting tables; he had earned all of the money that would take care of him for the rest of the year. He used to talk with me and tell me that Brown was wonderful. That piqued my interest.

Besides Mike Stein, there is another person Tauro credits for his admission to Brown, in a back-handed way.

> *Joe Tauro:* There was a teacher at Swampscott High named Walter Henshaw, who went around one day in history or English class and asked everybody what they wanted to do next year after we graduated—sort of an informational thing. When my turn came I said: "I'm going to go to Brown

> University." Walter said in front of the whole class that the only way I was going to see Brown University was if I went down there to visit somebody. I thought to myself: Oh yeah? We'll see.
>
> Later, when the college acceptances came out, I was walking down the corridor when I ran into Walter, who was talking with a kid who had not gotten into Brown. When I walked by, instead of saying congratulations, he looked at me and said: "I guess some people just have the right handshake, don't they?" I just kept walking. That was his way of saying I had gotten lucky and didn't deserve to get in on merit. That's why Walter Henshaw is one of the people I put down as a reason for my success.

The real key to Tauro's admission to Brown, however, was the Swampscott principal, James Dunn.

> *Joe Tauro:* I found out later how much Mr. Dunn had helped. When I was a senior at Brown and applying to law school, I went to see the vice-president at Brown to ask for a recommendation. He pulled my file and as he looked through it, he asked me: "How well did you know this Jim Dunn, your high school principal?" He said it was amazing the way Dunn had pushed me and put everything on the line for me. He told me I never would have gotten into Brown without Dunn going out on a limb for me. Mr. Dunn had just taken a liking to me. I think he was fascinated by the fact that I had shown up for just a year and had become President of the Student Council. I will never forget Mr. Dunn.

Tauro loved Brown from the start. He became an English major and took every English course he could.

> *Joe Tauro:* I took something like 17 English courses, which you weren't supposed to do. I was pretty good at it and started to get good marks. My favorite English professor was Elmer Blistein. He was excellent. One of the courses he taught was creative writing, which I enjoyed. It fit in with my ever-increasing interest in show business.

Brown University baseball team; Tauro is in the back row, third from right.

COURTESY OF HON. JOSEPH L. TAURO

Tauro played baseball at Brown, where his coach, Lefty Lefebre, moved him to the outfield.

> *Joe Tauro:* I loved Coach Lefebre, but I didn't have the success in the outfield that I enjoyed at second base in high school. I always thought I was too much of a pepper pot for such a sedentary position.

Unexpectedly, a sport that Tauro didn't know the first thing about, soccer, also became a big part of his life at Brown, right from the start.

> *Joe Tauro:* I had nothing to do one afternoon during the first week or so of college, so I wandered over to the athletic fields to watch the teams practice. While I was watching the soccer team practice, I turned to a man in a sweatsuit standing next to me and asked him how many points it was when you kick a goal. Obviously I knew nothing about soccer. We got talking, and I went on to embellish a bit about my abilities as a second baseman, saying I was looking forward to playing baseball for Brown in the spring. The man introduced himself. He was the head soccer coach, Joe Kenaway, former major league soccer player from Scotland. Kenaway told me that he needed another freshman goalie and asked me if I wanted to try out. He said that playing goalie was a lot like playing second base—

you needed to have good hands and be quick. He told me he could teach me what I needed to know.

To make a long story short, it all worked out. I eventually became the starting freshman and varsity goalie for Brown. That was a great experience, and made me feel at home on the campus.

Playing on the soccer team led indirectly to another extracurricular highlight of Joe Tauro's Brown experience: serving as chair of the Interfraternity Governing Board Ball, a major campus event. While he was at soccer practice, he was asked by a committee of the Interfraternity Governing Board to take on that assignment. The request came with the admonition that Brown wasn't going to have a big-name band that year because they had lost money having Johnny Long, a big-name bandleader, the previous year. Tauro turned down the request, saying that if he was going to be chair, he would run the dance his way or not at all. Eventually his student colleagues saw it his way and asked him to serve.

Joe Tauro playing goalie at Brown in a 1952 game against West Point

COURTESY OF HON. JOSEPH L. TAURO

Joe Tauro: Of course, the first thing I did was to work on bringing the number one band in the country, Tommy Dorsey and his orchestra, to Brown for the dance. I literally followed him all over the country until he agreed to play for us. I think I just wore him out. Having Tommy Dorsey then would be like having the Rolling Stones and the Beatles today. We got them there, and it was a major success. I still enjoy reflecting on the memories of Tommy hanging around in my fraternity house with my classmates. He was a great guy to us all. The whole experience served to increase my interest in show business as a career.

It was while at Brown that Joe Tauro decided to follow in his father's footsteps and become a lawyer. Tauro says he made the decision once he realized that he would never be able to hit major league pitching, even in his dreams.

There was also a moment of show-biz doubt, though, when it came time to head to law school. Tauro had done well at Brown and had been admitted to Cornell Law School, but he wasn't excited about the prospect of going there.

> *Joe Tauro:* The night before I was to go off to Cornell, I decided I didn't want to go to law school. I wanted to manage dance bands. In that era, bands were very big. I wanted to be in the business end of it.
>
> That night I went in to tell my father about my change of heart. He and my mother were in bed, and my father was reading Time Magazine, as he used to do. I told my father that law school wasn't going to work out. I had decided that I didn't want to be a lawyer and I didn't want to go to law school. I wanted to manage dance bands. My father looked at me and he said two words: "Don't go." Then he went back to

Tauro's uncle, Tony Pastor, leading his well-known big band. With him are the Clooney sisters, Rosemary (right) and Betty, whom Tony discovered. Possible nepotism issues had prevented Tauro from hiring Pastor and his band for the senior dance at Brown. Uncle Tony was always a big influence on Tauro.

COURTESY OF HON. JOSEPH L. TAURO

reading his magazine. I was looking for an argument and thinking we would be staying up all night discussing my future, but that didn't happen. The next morning off I went.

My father knew I was going to go, and he wasn't going to get all excited about it. He knew I was a dreamer who didn't see himself as being a workaday world guy.

Cornell Law School

Once Joe got to Cornell in the fall of 1953, his qualms about law school and becoming a lawyer faded quickly. He enjoyed law school from the start.

> *Joe Tauro:* There were about 125 students per class at Cornell, and only about 375 in the whole law school. Class sizes were small, and there was a friendly, intimate atmosphere. If you had a question, you just raised your hand and asked it. It was a beautiful place with a terrific law school facility. They even had a squash court where I went almost every day at 4:30 or 5:00 to get revived after a day in class. Except for the cold winters, Cornell seemed to me to be the perfect place to go to law school. I loved it there.

Of course, law school was not all friendly and relaxed. One of the rites of passage for most first-year students at Cornell, as at many other law schools, was to survive a course with the intimidating professor that each section always seemed to have. By this point Tauro was confident enough so the experience didn't cow him.

> *Joe Tauro:* We had Peter Ward, who was a very tough professor. He was going to make me a man. He was a very successful young lawyer who had come in from Buffalo to teach torts. He had a big Cadillac convertible. What professor did that? Peter Ward worked hard. His lectures were good and his classes were stimulating. Everybody used to sit in the library thinking that maybe Peter Ward would pass by and grunt hello.

When the mid-semester exam came, we were given a fact pattern to analyze, and the theory of my answer was trespass ab initio. I got a B-minus on the exam, which was a good grade in those days. When he handed the exams back, Professor Ward announced that I was the only one who had discussed trespass ab initio, which was a compliment to me. Then later as he was going on about something else, I raised my hand and asked a question about the exam or some other theory. He turned to me and said: "Tauro, you didn't say anything about that in your exam. Why are you asking that now?" He really shut me down.

I was angry so I went and found him after class. I told him: "Professor, I asked a question and you blew it off like I was just trying to kiss your ass. I want you to know that I wouldn't kiss your ass or anybody else's."

He said to me: "OK, Tauro, I'm glad you didn't keep it in your crotch. Anything else you want to say?" I said no, that was it. He said OK and went on his way.

Later, I told my father what I did and he almost fainted over the phone. He said to me: "Do you realize that they could have thrown you out of there and that could have meant your whole career was ruined?" Peter Ward and I became great friends after that. He came to my first wedding. All the professors at Cornell were terrific, but he stands out.

CHAPTER 3

Military Service and Marriage

Tauro joined the R.O.T.C. while at Brown, and after he graduated from Cornell Law School and passed the Massachusetts bar exam, he went into the Army for two years as a lieutenant. He was stationed in Texas and Virginia. In Virginia, Tauro was the Launching Control Officer at the anti-aircraft Nike guided missile site. His outfit's mission was the air defense of Washington, D.C. Serving in the Army was a great experience.

Tauro with guided missiles at Lorton, Virginia

COURTESY OF HON. JOSEPH L. TAURO

Joe Tauro: I had about 130 men under my command, and I grew to realize what a responsibility I had to them. They were mostly just kids, and they expected me to know everything, including why they didn't get any mail. I really grew and matured during my two years of active duty. My confidence and judgment developed in ways that served me well for the rest of my life.

While in the army, Joe met the woman who would become his first wife, Elizabeth Quinlan. He was a guided missile officer, and she was going to Trinity College in Washington, D.C. On February 17, 1959, with Joe just out of the Army and working as a lawyer, and Liz out of college and working as a teacher, they were married at Liz's family home in Hempstead, Long Island. Before long, they began a family, which included Joe Jr., Elizabeth (Beth), and Christopher.

The Tauros raised three children together successfully, but the marriage itself did not stand the test of time.

Joe Tauro: Liz was a wonderful person. We got along well, and we got married. If there was a problem you could foresee it was that we got engaged a year after we met. We really didn't know each other. In those days people did that. One good thing about the way they do it today: they know each other. They know how they fold the towels; they know how they do the toothpasteall the little irritants that can break up a marriage. We just didn't know each other that well.

Tauro's armed services card

COURTESY OF
HON. JOSEPH L. TAURO

CHAPTER 4

Practicing Law

When Tauro was discharged from the Army as a first lieutenant in 1958, he went into practice with his dad, who had grown to be a successful and respected practitioner with an office in Lynn, Massachusetts.

> *Joe Tauro:* Dad told me my salary would be $50.00 per week. I told him that would be fine, but asked him how he decided on that number. His response was: "Your mother would kill me if I gave you any less."

The senior Tauro was a terrific lawyer and tough advocate, but a kind gentleman when he wasn't in combat.

> *Joe Tauro:* No one prepared a case with the commitment to detail that he did. Once in combat mode, he was tenacious. He practiced what he said was the Tauro family creed: "Never quit, ever."

Portrait of J. Newton Esdaile

COURTESY OF
HON. JOSEPH L. TAURO

Tauro learned from watching his dad, but Tauro Sr. wasn't a real teacher. He did not have the patience to teach, as did his Boston University classmate of 1927, J. Newton Esdaile. Newt was a legend of the bar, with a national reputation for excellence. Newt loved Tauro Sr. and looked to him regularly for guidance and advice.

In those days, law schools didn't have trial advocacy courses. Joe Tauro's trial advocacy training consisted largely of being tutored by Newt Esdaile himself. In regular sessions over a two-month period, Esdaile took Tauro through a personal injury case he was going to try in Essex County. He went over every pleading and piece of investigation, explaining why he had done the things he had done and what his tactics would be at trial.

> *Joe Tauro:* Before this tutorial relationship started, Esdaile sat me down and told me: "I don't want to waste my time on this training if all you want in life is to be just another successful lawyer. I'm a killer. Your old man is a killer. I'll only help you if you want to be a killer too." I felt like the Notre Dame football players must have felt when they heard a pep talk from coach Knute Rockne. I assured him that I wanted to be a killer, too. I sat with Esdaile during the two-week trial of that case. I was so mesmerized by his presence and performance that I often forgot to take notes. His final argument was like poetry, and the jury responded. That began a close relationship that lasted 50 years, until his death. He was a great teacher and a wonderful and treasured mentor and friend.

Mike Mone was another Esdaile protégé. Mone eventually became a law partner with Esdaile, and then went on to become one of Boston's leading plaintiff's lawyers as well as a good friend of Joe Tauro. Mike remembers one of the stories from that case.

> *Mike Mone:* The trial was up in Salem. In those days, when they opened up a new session of the court there in the fall, there would be a lot of fanfare. Every judge would come in at the beginning of the month, and the sheriff would show up in his cutaway coat with his staff. They would have a priest or a minister come in and do an invocation before the whole jury panel that was going to be sitting there for the month. The priest got up and gave the blessing and when it was over Joe blessed himself and looked over and saw that Newt was blessing himself too. Joe said to him afterward: "I didn't know that

Mike Mone

COURTESY OF MICHAEL E. MONE

> you were a Catholic," and Newt answered: "I'm not, but most of that jury is."

Tauro's work at his father's firm was interrupted by a fortuitous circumstance. During his freshman orientation week at Brown, Tauro had met a fellow student named Chuck Colson, and they became great friends. Colson later went on to become a successful lawyer and an important political figure. In the late 1950s, he was the top aide to U.S. Senator Leverett Saltonstall of Massachusetts. Salty was a Republican from a family with long roots in Massachusetts politics. Colson called Tauro in late 1959 to tell him that the U.S. attorney for Massachusetts, Elliot Richardson, was not satisfied with the applicants he had for an open position as an assistant U.S. attorney (AUSA). Colson asked Tauro if he would be interested in the job. After obtaining his father's approval, Tauro said yes, had an interview with Richardson, and was offered the position.

Richardson left salary negotiations to Andrew Caffrey, his first assistant. Caffrey would later become a federal judge, and Tauro's colleague on the bench. He was well known, right up until the time of his death, as being notoriously tight with a buck.

> *Joe Tauro:* I told Caffrey what my salary was with my dad—$125 per week—and that I would want a raise, if anything. Caffrey said that the salary would be $6,000, period. I checked my tongue and merely replied: "That would be fine." Over the years, I enjoyed reminding Drew about how tough he was on me, a young lawyer.

The U.S. Attorney's office in 1959 was small, only fifteen assistants, compared to more than 100 today. Tauro connected with Joe Mitchell, an experienced lawyer who had a portfolio of significant cases including complex securities litigation.

> *Joe Tauro:* Joe Mitchell was very generous with his time. He assigned me a lot of the court and grand jury work. I learned a lot thanks to him. As a new AUSA, it ordinarily would have taken months to accumulate an interesting caseload of the sort he gave me. Years later, during my tenure as Chief Legal Counsel to Governor Volpe, I had the opportunity to

recognize Joe Mitchell by strongly supporting his appointment by Governor Volpe as counsel to the Commonwealth's Commission of Administration and Finance and later as justice of the Massachusetts Superior Court.

During his time as AUSA, Tauro developed a strong relationship with U.S. Attorney Elliott Richardson. Later, as chief legal counsel to Governor Volpe, and as U.S. Attorney for Massachusetts, Tauro worked closely with Richardson, who served as lieutenant governor and later as attorney general of the Commonwealth.

Elliot Richardson

SOURCE: U.S. DEPARTMENT OF COMMERCE WEB SITE

> *Joe Tauro:* Elliott was one of the brainiest and most focused persons I've ever met. I particularly remember one piece of sage advice he gave me while puffing on his usual after-lunch cigar. He said: "Don't ever take a job just because you think it might get you a different job. It may turn out that you don't get the other job and then you will have lost twice."

The Volpe Years

Tauro's stay as an AUSA was interrupted after only a year when John Volpe defeated Joe Ward for governor in November 1960. It was a tight race in which Volpe overcame a high Democratic turnout fueled by John F. Kennedy's successful run for president. Tauro's father had represented Volpe's construction company and had long been close to him. Volpe named Tauro Sr. as his chief legal counsel, and Joe Tauro promptly joined his father's staff as assistant legal counsel.

> *Joe Tauro:* I was as green as they come. Shortly after we took office, the Governor sent for me and told me he wanted to file that day a special message to the legislature raising the salary of Supreme Court Justice Paul Kirk. I said, "Right away, Governor." I left his office bewildered. My father wasn't

Joe Tauro, John Volpe, and Elliot Richardson

COURTESY OF HON. JOSEPH L. TAURO

> around, and I didn't know who to ask. I wandered into the Clerk's Office of the House of Representatives and told the man on duty my problem. I had to write a special message but I didn't even know what a special message was. The clerk was very kind, explained the whole process to me, gave me forms to follow as precedents—and as I recall it, even typed up the message and legislation for me. In baseball parlance, I "slid in under the tag" and gave the Governor what he wanted on time, thanks to that clerk.

As it turned out, Joe's boss got a new job: Governor Volpe appointed G. Joseph Tauro as a justice of the Massachusetts Superior Court. It was the beginning of a distinguished career as a judge. The next year, 1962, Volpe appointed Tauro Sr. as Chief Justice of the Superior Court, and then in 1970, Governor Francis Sargent appointed him Chief Justice of the Supreme Judicial Court, Massachusetts' highest court, a position he held until his mandatory retirement in 1976. Tauro Sr. is the only person ever to have served as Chief Justice of both the Massachusetts Superior Court and the Supreme Judicial Court.

> *Joe Tauro:* My dad had a reverence for the bench unmatched by any I have ever seen. He loved being a judge and he loved the court.

After his dad went on the bench, Joe Tauro went back to practicing law full time. He kept as much of his dad's practice as he could and formed a partnership with his dad's long-time associate, Samuel H. Jaffee.

> *Joe Tauro:* Sam Jaffee was more of a business lawyer than a trial lawyer. If he had civil trial work of any consequence, he gave it to my father. He and my father were associates, not partners, but when it came time for me to join with Sam, my father told me that I couldn't stay in the same relationship with Jaffee that my father had because Sam was so much older and more established than me and that his reputation would bury me. No one would believe that I was more than an employee. We needed to be partners and we should call the firm Jaffee and Tauro, not Tauro and Jaffee. We presented the idea to Sam and he thought it was a good idea. My father gave me a checkbook and put $5,000 in it to get me started and make sure I had some money to pay the bills.
>
> For some reason, I just assumed we would be successful. I was 28 or 29 years old and I didn't know any better. As I look back, I realize that you can't just start a law firm—you have to have clients—but I didn't think like that. We just started and it worked out well. We had a well-rounded business and litigation practice.

They did well right from the start. Practicing law was an all-consuming job for Tauro.

> *Joe Tauro:* It was seven days a week. Everything I did was in furtherance of my law practice. Every place I went I was looking for a client or trying to learn something. I loved being a lawyer and having the responsibility to stand up for people who needed my help.

Joe, ever the baseball enthusiast, particularly enjoyed representing two Red Sox stars, Tony Conigliaro and Carl Yastrzemski. Joe and Tony were particularly close. Joe saw Tony as the kid brother he never had. There was a big age difference between them, but they enjoyed each other's company. Tony often dropped in to Joe's office unannounced, hoping to entice him into playing hooky and going out for a pizza or a sausage sandwich, both Conigliaro favorites.

One of those surprise visits was particularly memorable. Tony came in and gave Joe the very first "Tony Conigliaro Louisville Slugger." Joe was deeply touched by the gift.

> *Joe Tauro:* I told Tony how grateful I was, and that I would keep the bat in my office until one day I would give it to the Hall of Fame as part of Tony's exhibit. And Tony was on his way to a Hall of Fame career. He had hit over 100 home runs by the time he was 20, and seemed unstoppable until the day he got beaned in a game. He was never the same after that. I was the only non-family member permitted to see him at the hospital. His eyeball looked like it was sunk in the middle of his skull, and he was lucky to be alive.

Many months later, Tony came to Joe's home as a surprise visitor to his son Joe on his birthday. Tony asked to see Joe privately, and requested his car keys.

> *Joe Tauro:* I gave him my keys, he tossed them back to me—and I caught them. Then he asked me to shut my left eye and catch the keys. I missed. The keys fell to the floor. Tony said, "That's me. I can't see out of my left eye."

The question was how to handle it with the Red Sox. Eventually they gave him a shot at coming to spring training as a pitcher. During training, however, he realized that if he turned his head a bit, he could see pitched balls much better. This is what he did, and went on to a couple of fairly successful seasons with the

Tony Conigliaro, Joe Tauro, Volpe chief of staff Anthony DeFalco, and Carl Yastrzemski

COURTESY OF HON. JOSEPH L. TAURO

Red Sox and California. Finally, he reached the point he couldn't see well enough to hit big-league pitching, so he quit, hoping to have a career as a baseball commentator.

> *Joe Tauro:* As if he hadn't had enough tough luck, he then had a debilitating stroke that required him to have constant care for the rest of his life.
>
> I visited Tony at least once a week until he passed away, always looking for some sign of recognition. But that never came. It was a tragic loss of a man whose baseball career had started with such great promise, and to me the tragic loss of a friendship that I cherished.

In 1962, Governor Volpe lost his bid for reelection to Endicott "Chub" Peabody in one of the closest elections in Massachusetts history.

> *Joe Tauro:* I think the people running the campaign were so sure they had a winner that they kept everything in a very closed circle and did not run an effective campaign. It was so disappointing to me to see Volpe lose like that. I loved the guy and I cried like a baby when he lost.

In 1964, Volpe was ready to attempt a comeback. Joe Tauro had become close to Volpe during his two years out of office, taking his father's place as general counsel to Volpe's thriving construction firm, and meeting with Volpe frequently on a variety of matters.

> *Joe Tauro:* My father told me: I can't give you Volpe, you are going to have to earn him. He got me the entrée, but I had to take it from there. Volpe and I always got along well. I was not very experienced, but I had good judgment and he liked the advice I gave him. We developed a close relationship. I was serving as general counsel to his construction company and he wanted to meet with me often.

One night Volpe asked Tauro to meet him at his home. With just the two of them present, Volpe told Tauro that he was going to run for governor again, and he was going to make the need for a limited sales tax the heart of his campaign.

Joe Tauro: I told him that I was happy he was going to run for re-election, but that I thought it would be political suicide for him to base his campaign on imposing a tax on the voters. I'll never forget his response. He said: "Joe, I've been governor. I don't need to be governor again. But the state has to be put on sound financial footing, and the only way to do that is by imposing a limited sales tax. If the people want to reject me for telling them what they need, so be it." I thought to myself: it's too bad the whole Commonwealth couldn't have witnessed our conversation because if people had seen it, the election would have been a shut out.

Volpe asked Tauro to oversee his campaign.

Joe Tauro: Volpe said he wanted me to run his campaign. I was thinking to myself, "How do you run a campaign," but I didn't say that out loud. If he thought that was where his confidence should be placed, then I needed to be worthy of that confidence. I told him I would do it, but there was one thing I wanted. He looked at me a little disappointed, like I was going to ask to be paid or something like that, but he said I could have whatever I wanted. He had a beautiful framed copy of the Bill of Rights, which Governor Nelson Rockefeller had given him and all of the other governors, and that is what I wanted. Volpe didn't even remember that he had it. He quickly agreed to give it to me, and I agreed to run the campaign. To this day it is in my family room at Marblehead.

I was in charge of strategy and Tony DeFalco was in charge of people. I would decide what we were going to do, and Tony would line up the people to make it happen. There were no rivalries and no backbiting. We were just a group of people who were very dedicated to putting Volpe back in office. Volpe was running against Frank Bellotti, who had beaten Governor Peabody in the Democratic primary. It was a very exciting time. We worked hard, making it a point never to close the office at night until we called Bellotti's office and they didn't answer.

The other thing I learned was to call a couple of reporters who were working at The Globe and The Herald every night around 10:30 or 11:00pm. They would be working on their

> stories for the morning paper. I'd call and find out what they were working on. Volpe had given me the authority to speak in his name, so I'd find out what Bellotti had to say on whatever they were writing about and I'd say: Volpe says such-and-such in response to whatever it was that Bellotti had said.
>
> That was late at night, but I was young so I was never tired. You would have had to explain to me what tired meant. There was so much excitement in the campaign.

The election was another cliffhanger, but Volpe prevailed. Volpe then asked Tauro to serve as his chief legal counsel, which Tauro did for the next four years. Tauro was paid only a token one dollar a year for his efforts.

> *Joe Tauro:* Each year the governor would give me my check for my one-dollar salary, always with the jibe that I was being overpaid. Being Volpe's chief counsel was the greatest professional experience of my life. It was like the television series "The West Wing." There was so much going on, and my adrenalin was flowing. It taught me how to face and survive enormous pressure. I worked closely with skillful lawyers and

Elliot Richardson, Joe Tauro, Ed Brooke, and John Volpe

COURTESY OF HON. JOSEPH L. TAURO

> political operatives like Elliott Richardson and Ed Brooke, who was our attorney general.
>
> We had to deal with all kinds of people, including those with odd ideas. I used to tell my staff to tell these people, or I would tell them myself, that they had a very interesting idea and they should take it down the hall to the Attorney General's office. Eddie McCormack had taken over as AG by then, and one day Eddie and his top aide came to see me.
>
> Eddie said: "You're telling a lot of people when they have a problem to come down to our office and these guys are mostly off the wall." I said yeah.
>
> He said: "You think it's funny? Let me tell you something. For every one you get, we get 20. You want to keep it up? I'll send all our special cases down to you." I said I understood, and that was the end of our sending people down to them.
>
> It was a job where you had so many different people and problems to deal with. Every day it was something different. My judgment sharpened on a daily basis. As I look back, it was the perfect training for going on the federal bench.

A collateral benefit for Tauro was that he got to know Attorney General Edward Brooke well. They worked closely together on many matters, and they grew to like and trust each other.

It was also a chance to meet many other political heavyweights, including the President.

> *Joe Tauro:* Volpe asked me to accompany him to a meeting in Hartford with President Lyndon Johnson. I was in a hurry to meet Volpe and got pulled over for speeding in the tunnel. The cop asked me why I was in such a hurry. I told him that I was Joe Tauro, chief counsel to Governor Volpe, and that the governor was waiting for me to meet him at the State House and accompany him down to Hartford, where we had an appointment with President Johnson. That's why I was in such a hurry. The cop looked at me and said: "I don't know if it's the truth, but it's a hell of a story. Go ahead!"

By the time the 1966 election season arrived, a Massachusetts constitutional amendment had changed the governor's term from two years to four. Volpe had

John Volpe, Joe Tauro, and President Lyndon Johnson at the meeting in Hartford
COURTESY OF HON. JOSEPH L. TAURO

been planning to run for reelection, but his decision became more complicated when Leverett Saltonstall, a Republican who was then the senior senator from Massachusetts, announced that he was not going to run for reelection. That left an opening for the Republican nomination, and led to a meeting between Ed Brooke and John Volpe.

> *Ed Brooke:* I asked him: "John, what are you going to do? If you are going to run for reelection, then I am going to run for the Senate, but if you are going to run for the Senate then I will make a decision as to whether to run for governor."
>
> He said he thought I was rushing to judgment. We had just heard the news, and he wanted time to think it over. I said to him that I didn't think we had time. There were a lot of people who were interested in both positions and a decision had to be made.

Joe Tauro: I was there when they met. Brooke said he would be willing to defer his own decision and to give Volpe 30 days to think it over and make up his mind. We put it on the side burner.

I had a mental clock in my mind focused on that, and when the 30 days was almost over, I went to Volpe and asked him what he was going to do. He didn't want to make a decision yet, but I reminded him of the agreement. He asked me to make a list of the pluses and minuses of the two positions, which I did. When Volpe asked my opinion I told him that he was an executive, and it was hard for me to see him being happy as a member of a deliberative body like the Senate where they make speeches and don't have executive authority. I also reminded him that if he did get elected to the Senate he would be the junior senator, in Teddy Kennedy's shadow, and Kennedy was likely to be there a long time. That impressed him and he told Brooke that he was going to run for reelection as governor.

For once, the election was not a squeaker. Volpe defeated the Democratic challenger, Edward McCormack, by a comfortable margin. Once again, Tauro had a key role in the campaign.

Leverett Saltonstall, G. Joseph Tauro, Helen Petrossi Tauro, Chief Justice Edward Hennessey, and Joe Tauro

COURTESY OF HON. JOSEPH L. TAURO

Volpe would serve only about half of his term as governor. The 1968 presidential election intervened, setting the political wheels turning again. Volpe was an early and outspoken supporter of the front runner for the Republican nomination, former Vice President Richard Nixon. Volpe ran in the Massachusetts Republican primary as a "favorite son," pledging to deliver his delegates to the Nixon column at the convention.

In the meantime, Governor Nelson Rockefeller mounted a late challenge to Nixon. Rockefeller struggled to gain traction in much of the country, including the south and the midwest, but in Massachusetts many Republicans supported him, including party leaders like Ed Brooke and Elliot Richardson.

> *Joe Tauro:* The primary was an embarrassment for Volpe. We just took it for granted that Volpe was going to win, and nobody campaigned. Rockefeller ran as a write-in candidate, and he prevailed. I was standing next to Volpe at the convention later when Governor Rockefeller came up to him and said he was sorry about how things had to go. Volpe said, "Well, that's politics. That's how it goes. Congratulations."

Meanwhile, Nixon was in the process of locking up the presidential nomination, while Volpe and his team, including Tauro, were in their own all-out campaign for the vice presidential nomination. It came within a hair of succeeding.

> *Joe Tauro:* We were in Cincinnati, Ohio, before the convention, after Nixon had the nomination locked up, when John Mitchell, Nixon's campaign manager and later attorney general, came out to meet Volpe at the hotel where we were staying. They were trying to size him up. Volpe was a serious candidate for the vice presidential nomination.
>
> Later I found out just how close Volpe came to being Nixon's selection. I was Volpe's surrogate at a high-level meeting in Washington some time after the convention. Senator John Tower, the powerful Republican senator from Texas, was there. The conversation turned to Nixon's choice of Spiro Agnew as his vice-presidential nominee. Tower had been the one who met with Nixon at the time of the convention to find out who the selection was and to report back to the

convention leaders. Tower said Nixon told him it was Volpe. When Tower reported that news to South Carolina Senator Strom Thurmond, Thurmond told him: "You tell Nixon that he promised us either a southerner or a border-state guy and I'm holding him to that promise." That's what caused Nixon to back off Volpe and choose Agnew, who was a border-state guy from Maryland. Later, I was in Washington with Volpe for Nixon's swearing in. At some point Volpe, who hadn't heard that story, came to me and said: "Something funny just happened. Senator Thurmond—I don't even know him—just came up to me and said: 'You know, John, it was never anything personal as far as I was concerned'." That exchange gave credence to Senator Tower's story.

Nixon offered Volpe a consolation prize: a Cabinet position of his choice.

Joe Tauro: He told Volpe: "You've got to be in my cabinet. I don't care what job you want, it's yours. You have to promise me you'll do it." If Volpe had wanted Secretary of State, that wouldn't have happened, but something like Labor or Commerce or anything that fit his considerable business talents was a possibility. We went out to meet with Nixon in

John Volpe, President Richard Nixon, and Henry Kissinger

COURTESY OF LUCIUS BEEBE MEMORIAL LIBRARY, WAKEFIELD, MASS.

> San Diego to tell him what Volpe's choice was. My advice to him was to go for Transportation. It was a brand new agency and it wasn't stodgy. It was going to be 21st century. Volpe picked that and it worked out well for him.
>
> While we were in San Diego I got a little taste of what my life might have been like if Nixon had picked Volpe as his vice-presidential nominee. I was walking down the street with the governor's press secretary, Barry Locke, when we ran into a nice, young Agnew staffer whom we had gotten to know over the years. We asked him how it was going. He said he'd just had to call his wife to ask her to send him some underwear. He hadn't had a chance to go home at all.

Volpe then asked Tauro to come to Washington with him as the general counsel in the Department of Transportation. Tauro gave it some thought, but in the end he declined.

> *Joe Tauro:* I would have had to give up my law practice and uproot my family, and the financial consequences would have been enormous. I decided to stay in Boston, but I wound up opening a Washington branch of my law practice.
>
> I was back practicing in Boston after the election when Chuck Colson called me one day. He said *The Wall Street Journal* was going to be publishing a big story about who were going to be the influential lawyers in the Nixon administration. They had called him, and he told me that I was going to be a part of the story. He had told the reporter that he thought I was going to be opening up a Washington branch and that I would be a big factor because of my past association with Volpe. I told Chuck that we weren't planning to open up a Washington office. He said: "Well, the guy's probably going to call you within the half hour. You've got a half hour to make up your mind. Say that you're going to open up an office and you will be in the story. If you're not, then you're not going to be in the story." The guy did call me and I told him that we were going to open up an office and I was a big part of the story.

The Washington office worked out well. Jaffee and Tauro arranged to share space with Colson's former law firm, Gadsby & Hannah, and opened for business. Soon Tauro had a couple of clients.

> *Joe Tauro:* Chuck Colson asked me how much of a retainer I had gotten. I said I didn't get a retainer. He said that at that rate I was going to be the busiest lawyer in Washington. Everybody asks for a retainer. So I had to go back to the couple of guys I had handshakes with and ask them for retainers. I think they were about $30,000 a year. Nobody batted an eyelash.
>
> We had some good clients. One was Allstate, which had hired us in connection with their campaign to persuade the President not to pursue a national no-fault bill. I did a lot of work on that. In the end we killed the bill.

Tauro was back and forth to Washington pretty regularly, but one trip stands out.

> *Joe Tauro:* I decided to take my family down to Washington with me on one of my trips and make a weekend out of it. We were going to have lunch or dinner with Governor Volpe while we were down there, but Volpe called and said he wanted us to leave town. There were huge anti-war demonstrations on the mall, and they thought there might be riots. President Nixon was up all night, talking to people, trying to calm them down.
>
> Liz and I decided to take Volpe's advice and leave town. We got everyone up and dressed early. When we walked out of the Mayflower Hotel where we were staying, the streets were empty but there were a couple of limousines and motorcycle cops. It was clear that something was going on. Just then Bob Haldeman, one of Nixon's top aides, came out of the hotel. I asked him what he was doing there. He told me the boss was inside and if I had a couple of minutes, he knew he would like to see me. I said that would be very nice. A few minutes later President Nixon came out. Haldeman said to him: "This is our good friend, Joe Tauro." I introduced Nixon to my wife and my kids. My father was then Chief Justice of the Massachusetts Superior Court and some people had been pushing President

Nixon to appoint him to the Supreme Court. Nixon said to my kids: "I know all about your grandfather and what a terrific judge he is. Some people want me to appoint him to the Supreme Court and maybe I'll get a chance to do that. You should be very proud of him."

Nixon wanted to give us something but he didn't have any pens on him so he had Haldeman ask us back to the White House where he had plenty of them. It was obvious that Nixon was exhausted so I said to Bob: "Why don't you just tell the President that you will mail us the pens so he can get some rest." Sure enough, in a couple of days, the pens arrived.

CHAPTER 5

United States Attorney

Tauro's work in private practice lasted just under three years. In November of 1971 President Nixon, on the recommendation of Senator Ed Brooke, chose Joe Tauro to be the next U.S. Attorney for the District of Massachusetts. On the surface, Brooke's recommendation of Tauro might have seemed surprising since the two had been on opposite sides of a couple of political battles in the 1960s. Governor Volpe and Tauro, as Volpe's chief counsel, supported Elliot Richardson, Brooke's unsuccessful opponent for the Republican nomination for Massachusetts senator in 1966. Two years later, in the contest for the Republican nomination for president, Brooke supported Nelson Rockefeller, while Volpe and Tauro supported Richard Nixon.

Edward Brooke

SOURCE: U.S. SENATE HISTORICAL OFFICE WEB SITE

These differences, however, had no lasting effect on the relationship between Tauro and Brooke, who had grown to like and trust each other. When Brooke won the senate seat and later found himself in a position to select the U.S. Attorney, he turned to Tauro.[1]

> *Ed Brooke:* When Joe was Volpe's Chief Counsel and I was Attorney General, I had extensive communications with him. He was very impressive to me. I read some of the opinions he submitted to Governor Volpe and the work product was exceptional. I had a lot of respect for him, and we became good friends. Later, when I had the chance to make the appointment, I thought he had the qualities to make a fine U.S. Attorney.

Tauro at first resisted the appointment. His law practice had flourished—the firm had grown from two to nine attorneys and had opened two branch offices—and the prospect of a pay cut to a salary of $24,000 a year with a family to support was not appealing.

> *Joe Tauro:* Brooke had my old friend Chuck Colson call me about the job. Colson was then working as Special Counsel to President Nixon. I told Chuck that I couldn't afford to take the job, but he wouldn't take no for an answer, always emphasizing how important this was to Brooke. He called me at home one Friday night and told me he'd call back on Monday to get my final answer.
>
> Then he said: "Joe, there's one thing I want you to think about."
>
> I said: "Chuck, don't make this personal." I thought he was going to lean on our friendship.
>
> Instead he said: "What I want you to remember is that if you say no, you will spend the rest of your life wondering what would have happened if you had said yes."
>
> My reply was: "You bastard!" The following Monday I called Colson and said yes.

Tauro sold his interest in the law firm and prepared to become U.S. Attorney. A couple of weeks before he was to be sworn in, Ed Brooke called Tauro and said he wanted to see him. They met at Logan Airport, as Brooke was scheduled to fly back to Washington. Tauro's instinct was that Brooke wanted him to know that Brooke was going to control who would be appointed as AUSAs. It was the right subject but the wrong message. Brooke wanted to talk to Tauro about making AUSA appointments strictly on the basis of merit. Brooke said that's what he had done as Attorney General. Tauro told Brooke that he appreciated the advice, and he would follow it.

A few days later Tauro got a similar call from Richard Kleindienst, the Deputy Attorney General of the U.S. under U.S. Attorney General John Mitchell. Tauro had gotten to know Kleindienst pretty well.

> *Joe Tauro:* He was a smart, easy-going guy, and I liked him. As an aside, he was the biggest chain smoker I ever met.

Kleindienst invited Tauro to come to Washington for a final chat before he was sworn in.[2] Again, Tauro tried to anticipate the subject of the discussion. His speculation was that Kleindienst wanted him to sign an undated letter of resignation that could kick in any time he wanted it to. The meeting turned out to be very different. After a little small talk, Kleindienst told Tauro that he was a potentially hot political property with a political future if he wanted it. Kleindienst said that the U.S. Attorney's Office was no place for someone with political ambition, and if Tauro ever got any ideas about running for office, he wanted him to resign. Tauro was impressed with the tone of the meeting, and it made him feel even more proud to be joining the Department of Justice.

Tauro was sworn in on January 6, 1972, at the age of forty-one.[3] The office he took over was a small one by today's standards. There were 15 AUSAs, each of whom handled both civil and criminal cases. Everyone tried his or her own cases and handled his or her own appeals.

Tauro felt that by and large they were an excellent team of lawyers, but he wanted to put his own stamp on the office. A few weeks after he took over, he had a meeting of all the AUSAs and talked about his plans and ambitions for the office. He also told them that it would be presumptuous of him to assume they would want to stay in the office under this new leadership, and that he was going to have an individual meeting with each of them. At that meeting they could resign or let Tauro know if they would like to be considered for reappointment. As it turned out, they all wanted to stay, and Tauro reappointed all but one. The process served Tauro's purpose of letting them all know they were now his appointments and his AUSAs.

The Tauros, father and son, at Joe Tauro's swearing-in as U.S. Attorney

COURTESY OF HON. JOSEPH L. TAURO

> *Joe Tauro:* George V. Higgins was one of the AUSAs. He was a terrific trial lawyer and a nationally known author. His book, *The Friends of Eddie Coyle,* was a bestseller and was made into

Joe Tauro, Peter Yeats (director of The Friends of Eddie Coyle), and George Higgins

COURTESY OF HON. JOSEPH L. TAURO

> a movie starring Robert Mitchum. He and I became great friends, a relationship that continued until Higgins' untimely death. Later, reflecting on that staff meeting, Higgins told me that he went back to his office, sat at his desk for a while, and then realized he had just been fired in a sophisticated way.

The individual meetings with prosecutors gave Tauro a chance to get a better handle on what each of them was up to, and in at least one case to reduce a caseload.

> *Mike Mone:* Joe and my friend George Higgins used to talk about the duck case. When Tauro was meeting with the AUSAs to discuss their caseloads, one guy mentioned that he had a case under 28 U.S. Code, Section such-and-such, and Tauro said to him, "I'm not familiar with that. Is it some kind of securities fraud or banking statute?" The guy said it was an Interior Department claim. Joe asked about it and was told that it had to do with interstate transportation of waterfowl. Apparently some guy had gone to another state and shot a couple of blue-billed ducks or something and brought them back frozen, and he was locked up. I think they had the frozen ducks in some refrigerator down at the courthouse. Joe decided that was not the kind of case he wanted the U.S. attorneys to be prosecuting and he told the guy to drop the case. "We're not going to be trying ducks up here."

Tauro announced that going after drug dealers and polluters would be top priorities. He and his office soon backed up that announcement by pushing up the number of drug cases by 40% and bringing a number of well-publicized cases against polluters of Boston Harbor and several Massachusetts rivers.

On one of the drug cases in which Tauro was personally involved, he traveled to southern France for depositions. The case turned into an opportunity to get better acquainted with two men who would later become his colleagues on the federal bench. The Assistant U.S. Attorney leading the prosecution was Larry Cohen, who would later be appointed as U.S. Magistrate Judge; and one of the defense counsel in France for the depositions was Walter Jay Skinner, who later joined Tauro as a district judge.

There were five federal judges sitting in Boston during the time Joe Tauro was U.S. Attorney. The court assignments were drawn by lot, but it seemed that one judge's name kept coming up on cases filed by Tauro's office: Charles Wyzanski. Wyzanski was an appointee of President Franklin D. Roosevelt who had already served over thirty years on the court, six of them as its Chief Judge. He was a well-known and outspoken liberal. In a series of cases before Wyzanski, the prosecution did not fare well.

The first was a case brought by Tauro's office against an Attleboro man on charges of evading the draft. The defendant's *pro bono* attorney, Verne Vance of Foley, Hoag & Eliot, challenged the indictment on the grounds that the Massachusetts law, which prevented people on welfare from sitting on juries, was a violation of the state statute preventing economic discrimination against potential jury members and also deprived the defendant of his constitutional right to be tried before a jury of his peers. Wyzanski agreed with the arguments and not only dismissed the indictment, but also invited other defendants in similar circumstances to file their own motions to dismiss.[4] On the appeal, which Tauro argued personally,[5] the First Circuit Court of Appeals

Charles Wyzanski: portrait by Gardner Cox

COURTESY OF THE U.S. DISTRICT COURT FOR THE DISTRICT OF MASSACHUSETTS

sided with Tauro's office and barred the district court from dismissing indictments on that basis.[6]

Shortly thereafter, Wyzanski was again in the news, criticizing Tauro's office for bringing a case against a woman accused of embezzling $952 from a federal credit union. Wyzanski commented: "This is a horrible example of the way the U.S. Attorney's office has been working. I do not know whether to convict the U.S. Attorney of inattention or incompetence, but one or the other seems appropriate."[7] Wyzanski suggested that the U.S. Attorney's office should move to dismiss the case, but Tauro declined the invitation. In due course, the woman pled guilty, and Wyzanski sentenced her to one day of probation.[8]

Two months later, in June 1972, Wyzanski again took the government to task, this time publicly blaming Richard Kleindienst and the Justice Department in Washington for prosecuting what he called "insignificant criminal business," namely, the prosecution of a Boston man for smuggling contraband books into the country from Cuba. Wyzanski announced: "I have been criticized for saying that the U.S. Attorney in Boston does not know what is important business. I would like anyone to read this record and decide what it is." Again, Wyzanski underscored his position with his sentence: one day of probation.[9]

A Mann Act prosecution involving a teenage girl transported across state lines for purposes of prostitution brought still more criticism. Wyzanski again complained of Tauro's judgment in bringing such a trivial case. Tauro had kept his mouth shut in the face of Wyzanski's harsh criticism, not wanting to exacerbate the situation. In the Mann Act case, however, he decided to write Wyzanski a letter a few days before the trial was to commence. Tauro wrote that he and Wyzanski had coordinate but different prerogatives and responsibilities: it was Tauro's job to decide who got prosecuted and Wyzanski's to preside over their trials. Tauro and his assistants held their collective breath wondering what Wyzanski's response would be. It was better than they could have hoped: Wyzanski called Tauro to his office for a two-hour chat that could not have been more pleasant or flattering. Wyzanski told Tauro how capable and smart he was and that the only other person that Wyzanski would have invited in for such a chat was Elliot Richardson.

Tauro told his father about the successful meeting with Wyzanski. Tauro Sr. predicted that Wyzanski would continue his criticism, and the prediction proved correct. When a bank robbery case came before Wyzanski, he again complained that the case did not belong in his court. Wyzanski felt that the defendant, who had no prior record, should have been prosecuted in state court rather than federal court. The result was another light sentence: probation, plus restitution of the amount stolen, to be paid back over time, without interest. The prosecution viewed the sentence as tantamount to an interest-free loan. It was the last time Tauro would be on the prosecutor's side of a sentencing controversy.

NOTES

1 Theresa McMasters, *Tauro to Be Named U.S. Attorney Here,* BOS. HERALD TRAVELER; James M. Shank, *Judge Tauro's Son U.S. Attorney Choice,* SPRINGFIELD UNION, Nov. 18, 1971; *Tauro Named U.S. Attorney Here,* REC. AM. (Bos.), Nov. 25, 1971.

2 *Tauro Family Proud and Happy,* at 1.

3 *Chief Justice's Son New U.S. Attorney,* BOS. EVENING GLOBE, Jan. 6, 1972.

4 Walter D. O'Leary, *Judge Invites Dismissal Motions,* BOS. EVENING GLOBE, Apr. 6, 1972; Walter D. O'Leary, *Jury Rule Out for Pauper Ban,* BOS. EVENING GLOBE, Apr. 5, 1972; *Pauper Loses Change for Jury Representation,* HOUR (Norwalk, Conn.), Apr. 5, 1972; *Wyzanski Hints End to Non-Poor Juries,* BOS. HERALD TRAVELER, Mar. 7, 1972.

5 *State Pauper Law Clarified,* BOS. HERALD, May 3, 1972.

6 *United States v. Andrews,* 462 F.2d 914 (1st Cir. 1972).

7 *Judge Complains About Wasted Time,* HERALD NEWS (Fall River, Mass.), Apr. 29, 1972; *see Judge Hits Trial for Mother of 3,* BOS. EVENING GLOBE, Apr. 28, 1972; *Tauro Is Rapped by Wyzanski,* NEWS (Gardner, Mass.), Apr. 29, 1972.

8 *Gets One Day of Probation,* REC. AM. (Bos.), June 3, 1972; *Woman Completes One-Day Probation,* ENTERPRISE (Brockton, Mass.), June 3, 1972.

9 *Wyzanski Criticizes Officials,* BOS. HERALD TRAVELER, June 24, 1972.

CHAPTER 6

Appointment to the Massachusetts Federal Court

In the summer of 1972, just half-way through Tauro's first year as U.S. Attorney, three vacancies opened up on the Massachusetts federal court. As a forty-one-year-old freshman U.S. Attorney, Tauro did not expect to be considered for any of these appointments, but Ed Brooke felt otherwise. He called Tauro and told him that he wanted to nominate him for one of the vacancies.

> *Ed Brooke:* In my time as senator I had the chance to nominate four people for the federal court in Massachusetts: Levin Campbell, Frank Freedman, Joe Tauro, and Walter Skinner. When I was making a nomination I would look at their allegiance to the rule of law, their judicial temperament, their scholarship, their objectivity, and things like that. I was very much interested that they have no evidence of any bias based on race, religion, ethnicity, sex, age, or economic conditions of defendants and claimants. Each of them really adhered to the policy and had those qualifications already. One of the accomplishments I am most proud of is the quality of the young men who agreed to serve the government in that way.

Tauro told Brooke that he was flattered to be considered and asked for a little time to think about it. After speaking with his father, who strongly encouraged his son to take the appointment, Tauro called Brooke back to say he would accept the nomination if it were offered. Brooke was pleased, but in the meantime, Wyzanski's criticism of Tauro had been ongoing, and in the call with Tauro,

Brooke asked about his problems with Wyzanski. Tauro explained his side of things. Brooke responded by asking Tauro to send to him copies of all relevant articles and proceedings. A few days later, Brooke called to say that he had read the material and didn't see how Tauro had held his tongue. Brooke had just sent Tauro's name to President Nixon for nomination to the federal bench.[1]

> *Ed Brooke:* Wyzanski was always in battle with the government, particularly in his later years. He was a very liberal judge who was in the media frequently. I thought Joe handled Wyzanski as well as he could be handled, if anyone could handle Wyzanski.

There was still the approval process to go through, which meant review by a committee of the bar association and then a vote by the U.S. Senate. The process did not go quite as smoothly as might have been expected.

> *Joe Tauro:* Judge Frank Murray was a great guy who was a good friend of my father and a friend of mine. Before he was appointed to the federal bench he had been an Associate Justice of the Massachusetts Superior Court at the time my father was Chief Justice. Judge Murray used to give me good advice and warn me about pitfalls. He warned me about my confirmation, telling me to keep my eyes open. He said: "It has nothing to do with you. The sins of the father come visiting on the son." In other words, my father's enemies would try to undermine my confirmation if they possibly could.
>
> As it turned out, Frank Murray was right, they did try. The meeting of the
>
> American Bar Association was in Chicago that year, and one item on the agenda was to consider the nominations of me and a man who had been nominated to another vacancy.

Portrait of Judge Frank Murray

COURTESY OF THE U.S. DISTRICT COURT FOR THE DISTRICT OF MASSACHUSETTS

> My father was attending the conference. At some point he ran into an attorney named Jenner, who was heading the committee reviewing the nominations. Jenner told my father that they had just been talking about me. My father said: "As long as you are bringing it up, do you mind telling me what was the result of your committee's discussion?" Jenner answered that there was no controversy about my nomination but there was some about the other fellow and rather than deal with that now, the committee was going to hold us both up until after the election.
>
> My father was very upset, and told Jenner that he felt that was extremely unfair. He then went to Bob Meserve, a prominent Boston lawyer who was then president of the A.B.A., and he told Meserve that if the approval of my nomination was held up because of concerns about the other guy, my father was going to resign from the A.B.A. at the meeting. Meserve agreed with my father that it would be unfair to hold up the nomination, and he went to whoever he had to go to to tell them to unloose my appointment from anybody else's, and they quickly passed it.

A few months later, on November 2, 1972, after his confirmation by the Senate, Tauro was sworn in during a warm ceremony presided over by Chief Judge Andrew Caffrey. Tauro was to fill the vacancy caused when Judge Francis Ford took senior status.[2]

> *Joe Tauro:* Judge Ford was a great guy who had always encouraged me throughout the years. He was 90 years old as he sat beside me on the bench, after I had been sworn in by Caffrey. During the ceremony he leaned over, squeezed my knee, and whispered as loud as a foghorn: "Joe, you wouldn't be here if it weren't for my legs. My wife can't drive me any more and I just can't get around."

All of the judges of the court were present, except for Wyzanski, who wrote a gracious letter to Caffrey explaining his inability to attend.

> *Joe Tauro:* The ceremonial courtroom was packed. I think the happiest person there was my dad. After the ceremony he

> hosted a luncheon for my family at which he and I toasted with a couple of 'twenty dollar martinis.' I think we were the only state Chief Justice/Federal District Court Judge father-son combination ever.

Tauro had just turned forty-one and given all his experience, especially during the Volpe years, he felt comfortable on the job. His colleagues were friendly and supportive. Judge Frank Murray was someone he particularly looked to. Murray was a good friend of his dad from their days on the Massachusetts Superior Court, and he had attended Tauro's wedding.

> *Joe Tauro:* One day Murray said something to me that bolstered my confidence. I had to come to his chambers to ask about how to do something or another. He said to me: "You've had enough experience. Think it through and do it your own way."

Of course, it was no accident that Joe Tauro had followed in his father's footsteps to the bench. The two were very close. On the occasion of his father's mandatory retirement from the Supreme Judicial court at age seventy, in 1976, Tauro commented on their relationship.

> *Joe Tauro:* We have an unusual relationship because he's actually my best friend. You always love your father, because after all, he's your father—but I like my father. He's a hell of a great guy. I can recall as a young lawyer practicing law with him. I asked a question. He was sitting behind his desk and he rose and said: "Come with me," and he took me to his big library. He said: "Look through this library and if you can't find the answer come see me and I will tell you." In junior high there was a period when I was an underachiever scholastically. I was in a slump. He snapped me out of it by letting me know without ever saying it that he was very disappointed in me. I was letting him down. It helped me get over it.

Tauro Sr. was a role model for his son as a judge.

Hon. G. Joseph Tauro, Supreme Judicial Court

COURTESY OF HON. JOSEPH L. TAURO

Joe Tauro: My father revered the bench and he was forever talking about the obligation of judges. He couldn't stand judges who were bullies. He told the story of the time when he was a young 24-year-old lawyer trying a case before a jury in Salem. At one point he asked a question, to which there was no objection, when this tough judge interrupted to say: "That's a stupid question." My father stopped for a minute, and what ran through his mind was that he really wanted to tell this judge a thing or two. But I had just been born and he thought of me back home and my future, and he said: "I'm sorry, Your Honor, let me rephrase it." My father had no use for that sort of behavior on the bench. He felt that judges who bully lawyers were cowards. He felt when you're sitting on the bench, you've got all the marbles. The power is too great to abuse it like that.

My father also had a strong feeling about total integrity on the bench. You were supposed to be totally honest as a judge, but it was more than just bare-bones honesty. You really had to dig in and understand a case. He thought there was no greater privilege than to be given the opportunity to sit on the bench and decide the fate of people, and you had an obligation to do it right.

The lessons I got from my father were good lessons. I remember when Judge Woodlock came on the bench he came around to talk with each of us, and one of the questions he asked me was whether I had any advice. I told him: "The only advice I can give you is to resist the temptation to be a bully. You don't have to be a tough guy or raise your voice in order to be respected. You have to have control of your courtroom, but you can maintain control and still have a pleasant atmosphere." I think it's important to let the lawyers do the best jobs they can and try their cases fairly freely, without worrying about you biting their neck off.

Michael Ponsor

COURTESY OF THE U.S. DISTRICT COURT FOR THE DISTRICT OF MASSACHUSETTS

Michael Ponsor, who clerked for Judge Tauro and later became a colleague of his on the federal bench, has a similar recollection.

Michael Ponsor: I remember one of the things Judge Tauro said to me once about judging: "I want everyone who appears before me to be able to take their best shot. I don't want them to be so damn scared when they are appearing before me that they can't get it out. I want people to feel that I am listening to them, and I'm not there to humiliate them." That was important for him, particularly since he could be quite intimidating when he wanted to be.

NOTES

1 *Freedman Judgeship Door Open,* TRANSCRIPT TELEGRAM (Holyoke, Mass.), June 30, 1972.

2 *New Federal Judge Sworn in,* SPRINGFIELD UNION, Nov. 3, 1972; *Tauro Sworn in as District Court Judge,* BOS. GLOBE, Nov. 3, 1972; *Younger Tauro Sworn in as Federal District Judge,* HERALD TRAVELER (Bos.), Nov. 3, 1972.

CHAPTER 7

The Family Business

With a father sitting at the top of the state's highest court while the son sat on the federal trial court, the Tauros were in an unusual situation. This relationship had an incongruous result in a handful of cases where Massachusetts prisoners brought constitutional challenges to their state court convictions: Tauro found himself sitting in judgment of decisions made by his father's court. Even though the Supreme Judicial Court was the undisputed arbiter of Massachusetts law, the federal court had the last word on constitutional claims.

In the three years that both Tauros sat on the bench, there were two cases in which Tauro effectively reversed the Supreme Judicial Court, granting prisoner petitions of *habeas corpus*. The first came during Tauro's first year on the bench. In *LaFrance v. Bohlinger,*[1] the prosecution impeached the trial testimony of an alibi witness through the use of a typed statement he had signed at the police station after many hours of questioning. The witness claimed that he had been repeatedly threatened with prosecution himself and eventually signed the

The Massachusetts Supreme Judicial Court in 1971. (L-R): Francis Quirico, Jacob Spiegel, John Spalding, G. Joseph Tauro, R. Ammi Cutter, Paul Reardon, Robert Braucher

COURTESY OF HON. JOSEPH L. TAURO

statement under coercion. Tauro held that the trial judge should not have permitted the typed statement to be used unless he found that it was not coerced; and that the trial judge should have told the jury not to consider it unless they too found that it was not coerced. Tauro minced no words in his feelings about coerced testimony: "Coerced testimony from any source is inherently unreliable and, therefore, suspect beyond redemption. Such testimony merits no consideration in the judicial process."[2]

Two years later Judge Tauro found himself facing another state court prisoner's petition which he felt had merit, this one challenging a conviction founded on evidence that the defendant claimed had been obtained in an illegal, warrantless search. In *Haefeli v. Chernoff*,[3] the evidence in question was an envelope full of stolen checks, which the police found in a car being used by a man and a woman whom they suspected were involved in a stolen-check racket. It was undisputed that the evidence had been obtained without a warrant, but the Commonwealth claimed the benefit of an exception to the warrant requirement in cases where there was a realistic expectation that the evidence would be lost if a warrant were applied for. Tauro disagreed, believing that because two police officers were present, one could have guarded the car while the other sought the warrant, and consequently the "exigent circumstances" exception to the warrant requirement should not apply.

Tauro did not allow the prisoner's petition directly, however. Rather, because it was not clear whether the presence of the second officer had been made known to the Supreme Judicial Court (it was a fact which the defendant-petitioner had argued and which the Commonwealth had acknowledged in the federal court proceeding, but which did not appear in the record of the proceedings below), Tauro deferred his ruling on the petition while directing the parties to jointly seek reconsideration from the Supreme Judicial Court. Tauro was signaling the Supreme Judicial Court his intention to allow the petition, while affording that court the opportunity to change its own decision first, before he acted. The Supreme Judicial Court declined the invitation, saying curtly:

> [T]his court did not consider "the fact that two police officers, rather than one, were involved in the challenged arrest and search," for the obvious reasons that the trial judge did not so find, and the parties did not raise or argue the point in their briefs or oral arguments.[4]

When the court stood its ground, Tauro followed through and allowed the prisoner's petition.

As it turned out, Tauro Sr. did have the last laugh on the *Haefeli* case. On appeal of Tauro's decision, the First Circuit Court of Appeals reversed, holding that the exigent circumstances exception did apply.[5]

> *Joe Tauro:* I remember one morning after I had written the opinion that reversed my dad— at least as much as you do in those circumstances. I said: "Good morning, Dad," and he said: "I got the mail," which was his way of saying he knew what I had done.
>
> When he told this story later, he would always say what a great thing it was for the integrity of the law that without any conversation between us I had done this—reversed my father's court. Then he would always end the story by saying: "Of course he was wrong." That was my dad's way of treating it and of letting me know that he was still Pop.

NOTES

1 365 F. Supp. 198 (D. Mass. 1973).

2 *Id.* at 205; *see also Judge Tauro Overturns Decision of His Father's Court,* BOS. GLOBE, Nov. 1, 1973.

3 394 F. Supp. 1079 (D. Mass. 1975).

4 *Id.* at 1090.

5 *Haefeli v. Chernoff,* 526 F.2d 1314 (1st Cir. 1975).

CHAPTER 8

Litigation: State Institutions

Belchertown State School

The case that would most define Judge Tauro's tenure on the bench did not take long to find its way to his desk. On February 7, 1972, a month into Tauro's tenure as U.S. Attorney for the District of Massachusetts, an attorney named Beryl Cohen filed a complaint in federal court challenging the conditions at a state-run residential institution for the intellectually challenged—the Belchertown State School. The lead plaintiff was Dr. Benjamin Ricci, whose son Bobby was a resident at Belchertown; the lead defendant was Dr. Milton Greenblatt, the Commissioner of the Department of Mental Health.

Up to this point, conditions at the state schools had gone largely unchallenged, with the notable exceptions of a couple of newspaper investigative reporting series, including an extraordinary nine-part exposé called "The Tragedy of Belchertown," written by James Shanks, which appeared in the March 1970 *Springfield Union*. Shanks' piece had begun to open eyes to what was going on at Belchertown, but it did not lead to change in the short run. Instead, the reaction of Commissioner Greenblatt was to fire the Department's Western Regional Administrator, Dr. Philip Wakstein, for disloyalty, because Wakstein had spoken candidly to Shanks about conditions at Belchertown.

Belchertown was part of a pattern. Similar miserable conditions also prevailed at the other state institutions housing the intellectually challenged, and nowhere had efforts to address conditions gained any traction. In the mid-1960s, *Boston Herald* investigative reporter Nick Gage went to work at the Fernald School in Waltham, the largest of the institutions, and then wrote a series of articles about the appalling conditions there. Nothing changed at Fernald either.

In the early 1970s, Ben Ricci and a group of other parents of children at Belchertown came to the decision that they should sue. The decision proved more easily made than executed, as attorney after attorney—more than a dozen in all—turned down the case. The plaintiffs had little money, and the case appeared daunting. Finally they found a lawyer who agreed to handle the case, Beryl Cohen, a former state legislator from Brookline. Cohen had recently left the state senate, while still in his thirties, to go into private practice. Cohen knew something of Belchertown, having served as the chairman of what was then called the Committee on Public Welfare, which had jurisdiction over legislation dealing with mental health, public health, delinquency, and mental disabilities. He had also read the Shanks articles and thus had an idea of conditions at Belchertown even before Ricci approached him. Cohen took the case with no written fee agreement, having been told by the plaintiffs that they would pay him what they could when they could, but that it was not likely to be much.

Beryl Cohen
COURTESY OF BERYL COHEN

Cohen and Ricci paid a series of visits to Belchertown to view the conditions there, and on February 7, 1972, Cohen filed a fifty-two-page complaint which recited a litany of appalling conditions at the facility and made claims for relief under both Massachusetts law and the U.S. Constitution. The case was filed as a class action on behalf of the more than 1,000 Belchertown residents.

Any momentum that the plaintiffs had gained in the process of preparing and filing the case was soon lost in federal court due to the luck of the draw, or actually several draws. The first judge to draw the case was Francis Ford. Cohen was thrilled at the draw, viewing Ford as a fine judge who had the courage of his convictions and would not be afraid to act. Cohen's assessment proved correct: on February 11, four days after the complaint was filed, Judge Ford heard and allowed the plaintiffs' motion for a temporary restraining order. Judge Ford commented: "I've never heard of such things. I never knew such things existed as the issues that were raised in the complaint."[1] The order he allowed was ambitious, requiring among other things that the defendants make a complete evaluation of the medical needs of each resident within 30 days, that they formulate a comprehensive treatment plan for each resident, that they fill staff vacancies, and that they formulate and implement a plan to obtain necessary supplies and make necessary repairs to the facilities.

The plaintiffs' euphoria at Judge Ford's order was short-lived, however. Judge Ford was ninety years old. He had befriended Franklin Roosevelt at Harvard and had been appointed by Roosevelt to the federal court in the late 1930s. His age was finally catching up with him, however, and not long after he issued the temporary restraining order in the *Ricci* case he announced that he would be lightening his case load by giving up his civil cases but retaining his criminal cases.[2] The *Ricci* case was reassigned to Judge Anthony Julian. Julian himself was seventy-two, perhaps a mere youth from Judge Ford's perspective, but old enough to step down from Judge Julian's point of view. Julian retired in July 1972, after a brief and uneventful few months as the judge on the Belchertown case.

The case was redrawn again, this time to Judge Levin Campbell. Judge Campbell was nowhere near retirement, and he quickly made his presence felt by allowing plaintiffs' motion for class certification. Not long after that, it was announced that President Nixon had appointed him to the Court of Appeals for the First Circuit. The *Ricci* case was again without a judge.

The case was assigned next to a visiting judge from California, Judge Manuel Real. It was hardly the sort of case a visiting judge could handle. Judge Real had the case for about six months and then eventually returned it to the court in much the same posture as it had been: the main events in the interim having been the submission of a proposed consent decree by the Attorney General's office, which the plaintiffs found insulting and rejected out of hand, and the defendants' motion to dismiss the case on jurisdictional grounds, which the plaintiffs opposed and the judge did not rule on.

In the spring of 1973, the *Ricci* case was reassigned yet again to a fifth judge, Joe Tauro. Altogether the first four judges had sat in the case for a combined total of just over a year, whereas Judge Tauro would be involved in the *Ricci* case, and in the related litigations that followed, for well over three decades.

Tauro read the complaint and decided to take a look for himself to see if the conditions at Belchertown were really as bad as the complaint made them out to be. His courtroom clerk, Austin Jones, called up Attorney Cohen, representing the plaintiffs, and the Attorney General's office, representing the defendants, to arrange for them to visit the school with the judge. Ben Ricci was also included in the visiting party. Nobody at Belchertown was to be told in advance that they were coming; the judge wanted to see the school in its ordinary operation. It was May 1973.

> *Joe Tauro:* When we arrived at the main gate I wondered if I had overreacted by arranging this surprise inspection tour. It was a beautiful day, and the campus was quite attractive with brick buildings and carefully manicured, rolling lawns. It looked like a nice prep school campus. I thought at the time: "This is a waste of time. What are we doing here?"
>
> Then we went inside. The conditions were even worse than described in the complaint. There was constant noise and screaming, half-naked residents lying unattended on the floor. Flies and mosquitoes flew freely because there were no screens on the windows, which meant that bodies of residents were covered with insect bites. There was clogged plumbing, unattended residents drinking out of the commodes, and an overwhelming stench of urine and feces. And there was just incessant screaming, almost like there was a soundtrack of horrible screaming.
>
> I spent nine hours touring every square foot of Belchertown that day. It was the most punishing experience of my life. I never saw anything like it.

> *Ben Ricci:* The judge informed us...that he had carefully read the fifty-two-page *Ricci* complaint and that he had a firm grasp of it.... He asked us to stay physically close to him "as we visited," in order that we would be readily available to answer his questions.[3]

> *Beryl Cohen:* I had made notes of the personnel problems and staffing issues in every building, so when we walked through I'd say to Judge Tauro and the others: "This is the third floor. This is where a 20-year-old resident fell through the window because there was no screen, and he either died or was

> seriously injured," and so forth. People were being showered on a slab with a garden hose, so instead of being in a shower with the water coming down, they were put on a slab, sort of like a mortician's slab, and washed with a garden hose. I can remember a room that had at least 30 or 40 people sleeping, naked, huddled against the walls. The staff had drugged people. There were terrible things that we observed.

> *Ben Ricci:* Judge Tauro wished to see the female residents' living area in "G" Building. The judge chose to walk up—as all residents were required to do.... As we neared the toilet area, Judge Tauro asked a male attendant to see "if we may enter." The male attendant went straight to the door in preparation for pushing it open.
>
> "Hold it," the judge directed the attendant.... "Has anyone instructed you to knock first and ask for permission to enter?"
>
> "No," came the reply, "besides, it's not necessary; they are low functioning anyway."
>
> "Beginning immediately," proclaimed the judge, "knock first and do not enter unless you are certain it is unoccupied or that there is a medical emergency in progress. And spread the word to your fellow workers."...
>
> [W]e entered the toilet area together....[There] [a] female resident seeking bladder relief was awkwardly perched on the wall-mounted urinal specifically designed for males.... It would be an understatement to characterize Judge Tauro as having been visibly upset.... Later we entered the bathroom and observed more closely the characteristic toilets without seats and the lack of partitions between toilets.[4]

Things got even worse when the visiting party toured the "K" building, which housed male patients who were considered incorrigible.

> *Ben Ricci:* As we walked through a dimly lighted corridor, the judge paused by a large metal door with an approximately four by six inch opening in its upper panel. As he peered through the opening, he was greeted by a gruff male voice, "Hey, you. Don't do that. The guy's crazy. Get out of there." Judge Tauro had peered into one of the several infamous seclusion rooms.

> A young, naked teenage male was sitting on the bare terrazzo floor alongside a once-filled metal army surplus food tray. . . . The so-called "crazy guy" had smeared much of his food, as well as his own feces and urine, all over his body, including his face and hair.[5]

At the end of the day, Ricci asked Judge Tauro if he could stay a few minutes more. He wanted the judge to see the graveyard. There Tauro saw that there were no tombstones, only small stones embedded in the ground with numbers and no names. Ricci said to the judge: "I know you can't do everything, but if you can't do anything else to help us, do you think you could at least get the state to put the names of the dead on their graves?"

At the end of the visit, Judge Tauro convened a brief but dramatic meeting of the parties, in which the Commonwealth's representative, a young and relatively inexperienced Assistant Attorney General named Terence O'Malley, found himself in the line of fire.

> *Ben Ricci:* [Judge Tauro] said, "Here's what I want you to do, without fail, tomorrow, Mr. O'Malley. Inform Governor Sargent and Attorney General Quinn that I visited here this day.... Inform Governor Sargent and Attorney General Quinn that I have seen the conditions, and they exist as expressed in the complaint.... But there shall be no trial. We shall achieve a consent agreement. Any questions, Mr. O'Malley?"[6]

> *Beryl Cohen:* We got back to the parking lot and he told us there would be no need for a trial because he had seen enough evidence. He collapsed the entire case right there in the parking lot. His view would carry the case for the next 30 years.

The judge's first law clerk, Mark Brodin, had come along on the tour. It was a day that made a lasting impression on him too.

> *Mark Brodin:* I rode out with the judge in his car. We both had read the complaint, but you take those things with a grain of salt, and I don't think either of us expected what we saw. The

ride home was very quiet. The judge was so moved by what he saw.

Joe Tauro: The law is very clear that if you take a view, and notice is given to everybody, then what the judge sees, or what the jury sees, is evidence, just as though you took photographs and marked them with exhibit stickers. To find the facts all I would have to do was recite my memories, and there was no evidence available to them to contradict what we saw.

I told them there was no possible expert testimony that could convince me that the conditions I had seen were the way it was supposed to be, so instead of wasting time litigating the impossible, why don't we go right to the remedial phase? I told them: "Let's see if we can start the world all over again, and without pointing fingers of blame at anybody, just come up with a consensual, remedial program that will put this institution closer to the 21st century than the 19th century." So with a little reluctance, because the state at first was not keen on this approach and it was a little like turning around a battleship, we eventually got focused on working out a consent decree and fixing the system.

In addition to telling O'Malley to inform the Governor and the Attorney General of what had happened on the tour, Tauro also spoke directly to Governor Sargent about the conditions at Belchertown. As Volpe's chief counsel, Tauro had been the one to recommend Sargent as Volpe's running mate in 1968 and the one to give him the call when Volpe made the selection, so, as Tauro puts it: "I had some credibility with Sargent. He knew I wasn't kidding." Tauro also spoke personally to Quinn, another man he knew well, about the situation.

Joe Tauro: There were many times then and later during the course of things that I had calls like that with public officials, always with consent. It was all right with everybody if I talked with anybody. There must have been a million places on the record where I made everybody say: "Yeah, it's OK if you talk to them."

Lengthy negotiating sessions followed over the next five months. Many long sessions, including some that ran all day, were held in Tauro's chambers with his active participation. It set a pattern that would continue for years, of Judge Tauro's close involvement with the negotiation and the implementation of remedial orders at the state institutions for the intellectually disabled.

> *Mark Brodin:* He kept everyone at the table. Sometimes he would reach into his pocket and send someone out for coffee and donuts while the negotiations went on and on.

> *Beryl Cohen:* He held all these sessions, sometimes weekly and sometimes more often than that. He was so specific. He would say in open court: "Look, I understand from the reports that there are no air conditioners and no screens in Buildings A, B, C, D, and E at Belchertown and for the past four days the temperature has been over 90 degrees."
>
> Then in front of a full audience he'd say: "Look, is the Commissioner here? Commissioner, stand up please. What is your name? Now Commissioner, I want you to file a report within ten days setting forth the steps you are going to take to provide air conditioning for the residents in those buildings."
>
> Or if he didn't think he had the guy he wanted in court, he might say: "I want the Secretary of A & F here next Tuesday, and we're not going to postpone it, so everybody has got to be here." He said to his clerk: "Do we have anything on next Tuesday at 11:00?" The answer came back that he had a sentencing at noon, so the judge said: "OK, next Tuesday we'll be here at 11:00."
>
> Then the word goes out to the Secretary or whoever it was—who might have been scheduled to go to Washington to testify or maybe he just wanted to go to lunch with his wife—that now he has to be in federal court.
>
> That person says: "Says who?"
>
> "Judge Tauro ordered you to be there."
>
> "For what?"
>
> "There was some issue about air conditioning at Belchertown."

> And the guy would say: "You've got to be kidding me!" There would be a little gnashing of teeth but the guy would show up.
>
> Tauro wanted somebody there with authority to answer to him and he's got such a nice way about him. He will not lord it over the guy when he shows up Tuesday at 11:00. He'll say: "Mr. Secretary, thank you very much. I know you have a busy schedule. We know of your interest in retarded persons— the guy may have no interest at all— and when you are done you can leave, you don't have to stay for the whole session. But I do have three questions for you to answer on the record," or whatever. So he gets what he wants.

On November 12, 1973, the consent decree in *Ricci* was signed. It was a gratifying day for the plaintiffs and their counsel, and also for Judge Tauro.

> *Joe Tauro:* In my remarks I said: "This is a very happy day for me.... I think what we have been able to accomplish here is to give some immediate relief to people who absolutely can't help themselves—those who are helpless in the truest sense of the word.... What this shows is what men of good will can accomplish and what the concerted effort of the executive and judicial branches, together with an informed and active citizenry, can achieve."

Monson State Hospital

By the time of the consent decree in the Belchertown case, the improvements there were in full swing, and they continued thereafter. Belchertown, however, was only one of a number of state institutions serving the intellectually disabled, and the other institutions were no better. Inspired by the results at Belchertown, parent and advocacy groups brought a series of suits over the next couple of years, modeled on *Ricci,* challenging conditions at the other institutions. These cases were characterized as being "related" to the *Ricci* case, and thus under the rules of the court each was assigned to Judge Tauro.

The pattern of the *Ricci* case began to replay itself. The next case involved the Monson State Hospital. Founded as the State Almshouse at Monson in 1852 and then renamed the Hospital for Epileptics in the late nineteenth century, Monson was home to people with a wide range of severe physical disabilities, ranging from epilepsy, to severe multiple sclerosis, spina bifida, and individuals without arms or legs.

In October 1975, Judge Tauro led a tour of Monson, this time accompanied not just by counsel and the lead plaintiff, but also by a bus full of about thirty people from state government, the parent group, and reporters. Tauro anticipated that he would need the support of the legislature to fund improvements that would likely be necessary, so he had invited all of the major political leaders, including Governor Michael Dukakis, Lieutenant Governor Tom O'Neill, Administration and Finance Secretary John Buckley, Attorney General Frank Bellotti, Senate President Kevin Harrington, and House Speaker Tom McGee, among others. They didn't all come, but most did.

As the bus was nearing the parking area at the facility that morning, it was flagged down by Speaker McGee, House Ways and Means Committee chairman John Finnegan, and Minority Leader Frank Hatch, all of whom had arrived early and who had already seen enough for their purposes. Attorney General Bellotti

Beryl Cohen, Joe Tauro, and others during a visit to one of the state facilities

COURTESY OF BERYL COHEN

had been there since 7:00 a.m. and also had previously toured the facility on his own a week earlier. Secretary Buckley arrived by helicopter with Senate Ways and Means Committee chairman James Kelly. The legislative branch had learned a lesson from the *Ricci* case: Monson was likely to involve another major commitment and needed to be taken seriously.

By now Tauro was using the media unabashedly, inviting newspaper and television reporters on the tour, as he would do many times.

> *Joe Tauro:* There was some criticism about taking the cameras out to these institutions because of privacy concerns. I remember a state legislator came up to me and objected. I said to him: "You're worried about these people, aren't you?" He said yes. I said: "Do you think they're better off with me doing this or not doing this? Do you think you could have the same impact with the legislature, trying to get things changed here?" He said: "No, you're right, Judge." I told him I was going to protect the identities of the residents and not photograph their faces. I wasn't cowed by any criticism over letting the cameras in. It was important that the public know what was going on. The public had to see this.

The bottom line of the tour was the same as at Belchertown. Judge Tauro called Monson "a human warehouse," and said that the kindest thing that could be said about it was that it was a disgrace.[7] Perhaps even more telling was the reaction of Attorney General Bellotti, who was disgusted with what he saw and announced: "After careful review, I have determined that this department cannot participate in a debate, however, well intentioned, that would serve to extend the current deplorable situation."[8] Bellotti wrote a public letter to Governor Dukakis stating his position.

Frank Bellotti

COURTESY OF FRANCIS X. BELLOTTI

Unlike most of those who toured Belchertown in October 1975, Bellotti had been there before.

> *Frank Bellotti:* When I was running for lieutenant governor in the 1960s, I used to travel all over the state. I visited all these institutions for the retarded, like Belchertown, the Paul Dever School, and Boston State Hospital. I did it because I had some

> interest in it, but when I went to the first place I was so shocked at what I saw that I went around to other places as well. The conditions I saw never left my mind. I felt that the level of care was not constitutionally acceptable. If you have a bumpy road, with potholes, people notice it. They get flat tires. Nobody notices the institutions for the retarded because you don't go in them, you go by them. You see the building and that's it. I always thought that something had to be done.

> *Joe Tauro:* Bellotti was wonderful. He came in and announced right away that he was not going to defend the indefensible. Then we got to work on the consent decrees.

Bellotti didn't have to do anything to persuade Dukakis to go along. Dukakis had missed the Monson tour, but he had been to Fernald years earlier, and he was in no mood to defend the litigation either.

> *Michael Dukakis:* When I was a second-term state representative from Brookline in the 1960s I was contacted by Harold and Charlotte Peterson, a couple of my constituents and supporters who had a severely retarded son at Fernald. They invited me to join them and some other parents and legislators for a tour of Fernald one Saturday. Kitty couldn't make it that day so I took my mother-in-law. She had spent a lot of time in Europe, and before World War II she had been a social worker in Germany. She had worked at one point in Spandau, which later became a prison where Nazi war criminals were sent; when she was there it was an institution for the retarded.
>
> The first building we went to at Fernald housed about 75 severely retarded boys. Many of them were sitting on the concrete floors in their own excrement. The back wards were just unbelievable. This was in liberal progressive Massachusetts in the middle of the "Great Society." As we were leaving, my mother-in-law turned to me and said: "Michael, we never had anything that bad in the Weimar Republic in

Michael Dukakis

SOURCE: LIBRARY OF CONGRESS, PHOTOGRAPHER: THOMAS J. O'HALLORAN

> the 1920s." I made a silent promise to myself then that if I was ever in a position to do anything about it I would. I didn't do anything about it for years after that—none of us did. Then I became governor and we were sued. Bellotti and I sat down together and he said to me: "I can't defend this suit. If you want to appoint a special attorney general, go ahead, but I can't defend it." I said to him: "I'm not going to defend it either. It's indefensible."

Thus Tauro now had allies in the attorney general's office and the governor's office whose approaches coincided with the judge's approach: forget mounting a traditional legal defense on the merits and concentrate instead on negotiating a consent decree and making the changes necessary to enable the institution to do its job properly.

He also had another ally, Speaker McGee. McGee had agreed to come on the Monson tour at the personal invitation of Judge Tauro.

> *Joe Tauro:* I said: "Tommy, you come out and visit Monson. I want you to go look at it. Then if you tell me that you see something different than I am talking about, I'll forget it. I'll leave you alone and won't ask you for any help. Is that fair?" We had known each other for years.
>
> He went and after he had seen the place nobody needed to convince him what was right. He told me it was even worse than I had said and he told me: "I want you to know that you can have anything you want." He kept his word. Whatever we said we needed, within reason, he would get passed. We treated him with respect, and he treated us with respect. I remember him saying to me: "I just think if we can't take care of these people, we had better fold up our tents and go home. We are not ready to do that. We are committed to the job that you want done. The people involved want it done and we'll do it."

Fernald, Wrentham, and Dever Schools

Soon there was yet another suit, this one challenging the conditions at the Fernald School in Waltham. Originally called the Massachusetts School for Idiot Children, Fernald was another of the state schools for the intellectually disabled, like Belchertown. With a campus of 186 acres housing up to 2,500 students in what at one point was a total of seventy-two buildings, Fernald was the largest of the schools.

The Fernald litigation began as the others had, with a court-ordered tour of the facilities, which took place in February 1976. The findings were predictable: dilapidated facilities and severe understaffing. There were inoperable toilets, wet floors, broken glass, and peeling paint. The judge was told that there was a new unit ready to open which could house 144 patients, but that it couldn't be occupied because there was no staff available to run it.

The verdict was much the same as at Belchertown and Monson: Judge Tauro called Fernald "a pigpen," and "a disgrace," saying: "You don't have to be a constitutional law expert to know what should be done about this place."[9] The next month the federal Department of Health, Education and Welfare chimed in, issuing a scathing report about conditions at Fernald and threatening to withhold $5 million in federal reimbursements if steps were not taken right away to rectify the situation.

The next month there was another suit and another tour, this one at the
t... and oldest of the state schools for the intellectually disabled, Wrentham,
h... o roughly 1,200 residents. Again it was a full bus leaving the federal court
at ... Office Square carrying state officials, legislators, parents, and the press.
Th... he state commissioner of mental health, Dr. Robert Okin, came along.
Ev... having done a number of these tours, Judge Tauro grew visibly angry
du... r. He said that he was "amazed, dismayed and shocked" at what
he ... Wrentham was "an absolute disgrace and a nightmare," worse
eve... rtown on the day of his first visit. At one building Tauro
com... building wouldn't pass muster as a jail."[10] Lewis Livermore of
the ... tration and Finance was along on the tour, and Tauro told
Liver... by as they went through the facilities. Dr. Okin agreed
that ... entham were deplorable. He left the tour in the middle

of the day to go to a meeting with Speaker McGee to discuss funding for the necessary improvements and staffing.

Reaction and Change

The state was learning as it went along, trying to react quickly and aggressively to address conditions. When Tauro returned to Belchertown in early 1976, the beneficial effects of improvements were evident. Facilities had been repaired and upgraded and additional staff had been hired.

A study of staffing levels at the state schools at the time showed the difference—Wrentham and Dever (another school that would be the subject of a lawsuit before Judge Tauro) were each judged to be understaffed by 500 people; Fernald by 400 people; at Belchertown the staffing shortage was down to only 120 people.

In June 1977, Judge Tauro led a return visit to Fernald to assess progress in the sixteen months following his first visit. Much had been accomplished. There was still much to be done to reach an acceptable level of staffing, but improvements to the facilities were striking. Fernald was no longer a "pigpen," according to Tauro, it was now a "clean warehouse."[11] A few months later, in appreciation for the judge's role in spearheading the improvements, the Friends of Fernald support organization named Tauro its Man of the Year.

Negotiations over the consent decrees for all the institutions in litigation proceeded concurrently with the improvements themselves. Judge Tauro kept the pressure on.

> *Joe Tauro:* Negotiating the decrees was a painstaking process. Collectively, we spent hundreds and hundreds of hours examining each of those institutions, building by building, position by position, resident by resident.

Nonnie Burnes

COURTESY OF NONNIE S. BURNS

By now there was another law firm, Hill & Barlow, representing the plaintiffs in the cases of Dever and Wrentham. Richard Renehan, an experienced litigator, was the lead attorney. Nonnie Burnes, then a junior associate at Hill & Barlow, did much of the work and would end up spending a third of her time on these cases for many years, beginning in 1977. Burnes later went on to become a Justice of the Massachusetts Superior Court. She recalls Judge Tauro's role.

> *Nonnie Burnes:* He would call meetings in his lobby and get everyone in there. Although he knew a lot about the facilities, he couldn't know the level of detail that the administrators did, but he had a good nose for the truth or evasiveness. When he thought somebody wasn't really telling the whole thing, he would lean on them.
>
> Pretty much everything was negotiated. Judge Tauro almost never had to make a decision. I think his brilliance in managing the cases was that he could have gotten completely mired down in the details—you need to have five more nurses here, or eight more physical therapists there—but he didn't let that happen. Instead, he kept the pressure on the parties to work out those things. He would always say: "Who needs to do what to whom to make this happen?" He would say: "How long is it going to take?" and the state would have to commit to a time. He made sure we never left court without a date to return.

Resolving issues through consent decrees had obvious advantages over the alternative.

> *Beryl Cohen:* Tauro was generally able to avoid serious standoffs with the legislature by drawing on his political acumen and experience. He understood the give and take of politics. If he were just another federal judge, he perhaps would have entered a lot more orders than he did. But those orders could have been appealed up to the Court of Appeals or higher, and he may have been reversed. Then the whole case would have been just something for law students to fool around with. He's a smart man, and what he did was twist arms, and make phone calls, and hold conferences in his chambers.

> *Joe Tauro:* I had frequent status conferences, where the parties would come in and tell me what they were doing, what they were working on, and what problems they were having in reaching agreement. If they couldn't work it out and I couldn't work it out with them, then I would decide, but that didn't happen a lot. My job was to get them off the dime and keep the project moving. That was my greatest value in the process. I didn't sit down with them all the time, day by day, room by room, but I made sure they were doing it, with the requirement that they would report back to me frequently, in open court, with the machine going and the court reporter taking everything down. There was constant pressure. They knew I wasn't going away and this wasn't going away.

In July 1977, a major milestone was reached. Consent decrees were signed in the four pending cases other than Belchertown (in which a consent decree had been entered previously). The decrees called for further staffing increases and facilities improvements beyond the major changes already achieved. Governor

Tauro Jr., Frank Bellotti, Tauro Sr., and Michael Dukakis

COURTESY OF HON. JOSEPH L. TAURO

Dukakis and Attorney General Bellotti came to court to sign the decrees, and there were congratulations all around.[12]

Execution of consent decrees was only half the battle, however. There was always the question of funding the large price tags the decrees carried. On this too, Judge Tauro kept up a constant drumbeat. In September 1977, just two months after the decrees were signed, the judge was quoted in the newspaper as telling Governor Dukakis that he would not tolerate foot-dragging on the $40 million in renovations called for under the consent decrees.[13]

A few months later Tauro was at it again, using his favored baseball metaphors, telling parents, lawyers, and state officials at a court hearing: "I'm going to continue to ride herd on everybody. We're rounding third base, and I'm not going to have anyone trip over the bag, or get caught in a rundown, or just plain slow down."[14]

The election of 1978 brought a change in the Massachusetts governor's office, with Ed King taking over for Mike Dukakis, but the positive momentum continued for a period. Governor King toured a number of the state institutions on his own, without fanfare, and in the summer of 1979 he joined Judge Tauro on one of the judge's periodic tours of Fernald, promising further changes there.

Funding Battles

A few months later, as budget pressures on the state intensified, the era of good will began to wane, and Tauro's patience began to wear thin. The state had embarked on a huge construction program at Fernald, and as a result many Fernald residents were moved temporarily to Metropolitan State Hospital, where there was no heat in large sections of the building, only occasional hot water, and cockroaches everywhere. Then at some point DMH Commissioner Robert Okin stopped attending the court sessions. At one session Tauro asked Linda Glenn, the Associate Commissioner for Retardation, where Okin was. "He's tied up," said Glenn. "Tell him to untie himself," responded Tauro.

Judge Tauro was serving on the Children's Hospital Board of Trustees at the time, and at one point he got Children's Hospital to do a management study. He enlisted David Winer, the hospital president, to meet with Governor King to discuss the recommendations concerning Fernald. More than once, Tauro threatened to close Fernald. He was using all the tools in his kit.

> *Joe Tauro:* There were economic hard times facing the state, and I could not order the state to appropriate money, but I could shut down programs and institutions that were not meeting constitutional standards. That was the leverage I had. There were some real battles, though, times when the legislature was cutting everything, and I was trying to protect the staffing we had achieved. Sometimes after we had an evidentiary hearing I might agree to some staffing cuts, but most of the time I disagreed.

One of the tensest battles over funding occurred in the summer of 1980. The Massachusetts legislature battled its way through marathon budget sessions just before its anticipated Fourth of July break. At the same time, Tauro fretted over the fate of the appropriations needed to maintain and extend the improvements at the state institutions called for by the consent decrees. On July 2, Tauro ordered Governor King, Attorney General Bellotti, and the Ways and Means Committee Chairmen of the House and Senate to court to explain why the funds had not been approved.[15] A newspaper article described one of the all-night sessions in the House that week:

> Early in session on Wednesday [July 2] Rep. J. Finnegan (D-Dorchester) was locked in his Ways and Means office trying to avoid two federal marshals who waited outside to deliver a summons. It had been issued by District Judge Joseph L. Tauro, who wants to see a number of state officials in his courtroom Monday to ask them why money has not been approved to comply with the mental health consent decrees. Noticing that Finnegan's predicament had forced him to miss a number of roll calls, Rep. Steven Karol (D-Attleboro) began chanting 'Free Finnegan! Free Finnegan!' He was soon accompanied by virtually every member of the 160-member House. Finally Finnegan's aide accepted the summons and Finnegan was freed.[16]

> *Joe Tauro:* I wanted Finnegan served with the summons. He didn't want to come to court, but he was a lawyer and he would not ignore a summons. I sent the marshal up and I told

> him: don't come back until you've got him. The marshal served him, and to his credit Finnegan showed up in court.
>
> In the middle of this period when Finnegan was giving me a hard time and not wanting to show up in court, I got a call from Speaker McGee saying: "What are you doing?"
>
> I said to him: "Did you ever call me when I didn't call you back?"
>
> He said "Never."
>
> I said: "Well that so-and-so Finnegan won't return my calls and is ignoring me."
>
> McGee said he would have him there in 20 minutes. I told him it was too late—I had already sent the marshals out and he was going to be arrested.

> *Nonnie Burnes:* Judge Tauro couldn't tell Finnegan what to do in his committee, and he couldn't tell him that he had to vote a certain way, but he could embarrass him, and that's what he did. The press was all over this because there were so many people involved. It was always good theater.

The summons to Tauro's friend, Bellotti, was no more popular and considerably less effective.

> *Frank Bellotti:* I was in the lobby in the McCormack Building, where the AG's office is, and a marshal came up to me and went to serve me. He said that Joe couldn't get the money from the legislature and he was serving me to appear before him. I said to him: "You tell Joe Tauro to take that summons and shove it. He has no jurisdiction over me and I'm not appearing in his court." Joe laughed about that later. He was just trying to lean on me, but I knew the powers that the Attorney General has, and I was not a party to that action. He was frustrated because the legislature was not appropriating the money and he was right, but don't summons me.

The next summer saw more of the same, as Governor King pushed a $5.1 million budget cut that resulted in significant staff cuts at the state schools. In July 1981 Judge Tauro issued a temporary restraining order banning scheduled layoffs of 400 workers at the state schools. Tauro relied on a provision in the consent decree stating that "prior to any decision to adjust staffing in any state school the defendants agree to consult with plaintiffs' counsel and to bring any disagreement before the court for its resolution."[17] He commented at the time: "Now we will find out whether the consent decrees are real or a political charade."[18] *Boston Globe* columnist Robert Turner wrote that "repetitive court battles over state funding of care for the intellectually disabled was described by a participant as 'like watching galaxies collide.'"[19] In due course, following hearings, Judge Tauro issued an order allowing the Commonwealth to cut 84.5 specified positions of the 408 that had been targeted.[20]

> *Joe Tauro:* Governor King was a real guardian of the fisc. I am a Volpe guy, and while he was a social liberal he was a fiscal conservative also, and he always left the budget of the Commonwealth in balance. I wasn't there to spend money unnecessarily, but I wasn't going to let them cut muscle. We had some hearings, and if they could show me where there was waste, fine, they could cut there. But most of what they wanted to cut I made them keep.

During the periods when the state's position was at odds with what Judge Tauro thought needed to be done, there was some frustration in the Attorney General's office with the way Judge Tauro was handling the case and with what some in that office saw as his arbitrary dismissal of their legal positions, such as their early position that the federal court lacked jurisdiction in the matter and a later argument that the judge was altering the terms of the consent decrees.

> *Nonnie Burnes:* They did not like him in this case and did not like the way he handled it. They didn't think he was acting appropriately as a judge. They felt he should have been doing the legal analysis and all that.

In the course of another bruising budget battle in 1983, Judge Tauro realized he had one other lever he could pull to try to get the outcome he was after.

> *Joe Tauro:* What I decided to do was to join the Secretary of Health and Human Services, Peggy Heckler, down in

> Washington, to make her a party. The idea was that there were federal funds involved, and they were not being properly spent. In other words, the federal government was not getting a dollar's worth for every dollar they were spending, and the money was not keeping these places the way they were supposed to to be consistent with Title IX and XIX requirements. I did it sua sponte, without any objection from Beryl Cohen.
>
> But the key was Bill Weld, who was the U.S. Attorney for Massachusetts then, and therefore had the job of representing Heckler. Was he going to oppose having her joined as a party in the case? He came to court the day we were going to have the hearing and he looked at me with that nice, big face of his and said: "The United States will have no objection to the motion, Your Honor." I said "Good." It was downhill after that. Peggy Heckler is a very shrewd woman and she was very good. She sent the message that if you don't do this, then I am going to cut off federal funds. That made all the difference in the world.

Tauro brought Heckler into the matter in May 1983.[21] In July, she threatened to cut off $20 million in federal Medicaid reimbursements unless the state appropriated the funds needed to improve conditions at the schools. In October, Secretary Heckler issued a report critical of conditions at the state schools.[22] Judge Tauro stayed action on the report to allow time for the state to respond, a strategy that appeared to be working for a time, as the governor recommended and the House approved funds to make the necessary improvements. The Senate balked, however, cutting 25% in committee from the requested funds. In December 1983, commenting that the pattern of responsible action had been "shattered" by the state senate, Tauro allowed a motion for protective order filed by Heckler, authorizing her to "confront the issues of decertification and the appropriate withholding of federal matching funds."[23]

When the legislature departed for the year without providing the necessary funds, Heckler renewed and escalated her threat, saying she would begin withholding $21 million to $32 million of federal funds within two to three weeks. Two and a half weeks later, on December 21, the press reported that Senate Ways and Means Committee Chairman Chester Atkins had bowed, agreeing to full funding at all of the institutions in question.[24]

A Shift in Focus

By this point, a decade into Tauro's handling of the cases, the primary focus of the cases had shifted considerably. From the time Hill & Barlow had filed the Wrentham and Dever cases, there had been a split in the plaintiff group between those who favored continuing improvements to the institutions and those who wanted to see them phased out in favor of devoting the state's resources to placing the residents in community residences. The Massachusetts Association of Retarded Citizens (MARC), which was an institutional plaintiff in both the Wrentham and Dever cases, pushed for community placement and felt that any money spent on the institutions was money misspent. The state was also pushing community placement. Some parents disagreed. In the case of many relatively high-functioning individuals, it was obvious that they belonged in community residences rather than state schools, but for other residents, parents sometimes felt that they would be safer and better served in the institutions. Hill & Barlow, which represented both MARC and the Wrentham and Dever parent groups, had to work to keep their clients on the same page.

Tauro thus found himself in the middle of a sometimes realigned dispute, with some plaintiffs and the state now in agreement. Tauro saw himself as neutral on the issue of community placement versus institutional improvements.

> *Joe Tauro:* My position was always the same: the intellectually disabled had to be properly cared for, whether in the community or in an institution, and until there were sufficient community residences available, the institutions would have to be renovated and provided with sufficient staffing so as to eliminate the existing constitutional deprivations.
>
> There was a system of individual service plans, or ISPs, for each resident of every facility. The ISP was a comprehensive thing that addressed the individual's mental condition, their physical condition, and what kind of effort could be made to rehabilitate them. If the ISP said that the individual could go into the community, that was fine with me. I would give permission for them to go into the community, but the first thing they had to do was to show me where they were going to go. I always wanted to know what was at the end of the bus ride. You don't just put them on the bus and have them end up in a motel some place. Then everybody started to realize

> how hard it was to find a place to send somebody. Nobody wanted the community residences to be in their house or the house next door—the old story of everyone being for something but not in my back yard. That's the struggle we had.

As the resident populations dwindled, the state began to close buildings at various institutions. In due course, two of the institutions themselves were closed: Belchertown (in 1992) and Dever (in 2002), in each case with the support of the parent advocacy groups.

By 1993, twenty years after his fateful first tour of Belchertown, Tauro felt the time had come to end the period of active judicial oversight, and he closed the cases. Care at the institutions, and the facilities themselves, had gone from being a disgrace to being among the best in the world for intellectually disabled patients. Tauro agreed to the disengagement order only after the Commonwealth committed to form a nine-member citizen commission to replace the judge in monitoring the performance under the consent decree and the quality of the state's care for the intellectually disabled.

Tauro's decision to close the cases was welcomed by the state, but not by the plaintiffs, who feared that without his presence there would be backsliding and deterioration in what had been achieved. In his disengagement order, Judge Tauro made plain that he understood the basis of the plaintiffs' fears and that if and when things did go downhill, he would entertain a motion to reopen and reinstate the case. He wanted the state to know that despite his closing of the

Joe Tauro and Bill Weld at the signing of the consent decrees

COURTESY OF HON. JOSEPH L. TAURO

cases, he would still be on call and would not tolerate the gains of the prior twenty years being jeopardized. Ricci remembers Tauro at one point saying: "I get out of this case when they put me in Landergan's Funeral Home. These are consent decrees. They never end."

The court ceremonies on the closing of the cases were marked by comments of counsel and of Governor Bill Weld, lauding Judge Tauro for his role as the catalyst in bringing about the extraordinary progress that had made such a difference to so many. It was an emotional event for many, including Tauro, who at one point broke down.

One of those offering Tauro a private word of praise that day was a colleague on the bench, Frank Murray. Murray had looked on with disapproval as Tauro for years had made such open and unabashed use of the press in trying to achieve his objectives.

> *Joe Tauro:* Frank Murray was a friend of my father and a judge I liked very much. Murray came up to me after the ceremonies that day and said: "I always thought it was improper for you to go to all of these institutions and bring along television cameras to stir up all kinds of coverage, but I was wrong. What you did was exactly what needed to be done. It wouldn't have worked if you hadn't done exactly what you did. I thought you were wrong, but I now tell you that I was wrong."

Murray's comment about Tauro's use of publicity was an exception to the general practice by judges of not discussing their cases with each other. Even though there were a number of other judges who had major institutional reform cases during the same time as Tauro's cases—the school desegregation case and the Boston Harbor cleanup case being two examples—the judges did not typically comment on each other's handling of these cases or share strategies.

> *Joe Tauro:* Everybody does their own thing. You shy away from saying anything because you wouldn't want anybody to think that you were trying to crowd the decision. Nancy Gertner gets a lot of publicity on her cases; she's like I was 20 years ago. She's flamboyant and not afraid to be ahead of things. I agree with a lot of the things she does, but I never say to her afterwards, "Good job," because then it's "Why didn't you say

> 'good job' on the next one? Does that mean that you thought it was a bad job?" It's a touchy situation.

One of those who closely followed the events in the Belchertown case and the related litigations was Bob Johnson, who later became CEO of Special Olympics Massachusetts. Johnson got his start at Belchertown in the period before the *Ricci* case was brought.

> *Bob Johnson:* As a young, optimistic college graduate intent on a career in Special Education, I entered the world of work through the doors of Belchertown State School. During the summer of 1970, I served as a recreation therapist there. Each day I would approach and unlock the front door of a dreary brick building and select 8 to 10 residents to take into a one-hour session, after which the residents were returned to the brick building where they would sit hour upon hour staring at the brick walls.
>
> One of my most vivid memories is standing outside the ten-foot-tall chain-link fence watching the residents of the adjoining building attempt to entertain themselves. They were grown men in various stages of undress with little or nothing available with which to be entertained. I remember clicking my tongue and thinking that there had to be a better way. I thanked the good Lord above that I did not have to face such an undignified existence. I was deeply saddened by the vision before me. I am ashamed to admit, however, that I do NOT remember feeling a need to do anything about it. I do remember the joy I felt when I read soon thereafter that Dr. Benjamin Ricci had been so motivated on behalf of his son that he had brought a lawsuit and taken on the system. I also remember feeling elated upon word of the consent degree issued by Joe Tauro. Justice had not been served but freedom had been achieved.
>
> More than 35 years later, as CEO of Special Olympics Massachusetts, I take great joy from the fact that I see people with intellectual disabilities living in the community, respected by their neighbors and friends and, in fact, quite skilled and talented in so many ways. Life is better but still not good. A "work in progress" is how I would describe it. However, if every generation makes as much progress as the

last two, I see a time when living conditions will be better; working conditions will be better; social conditions will be better, and healthcare will be available on the same plane with everyone else.

Ben Ricci and Joe Tauro changed the world forever for people with intellectual disabilities, and we have all benefited greatly from it. We are as inspired by people with intellectual disabilities as they are by us. We learn from them to take things in stride; to set and achieve reasonable goals, and then set new ones; we learn to be kinder to one another and, most of all, we learn the true meaning of unconditional love.

NOTES

1 Benjamin Ricci, *Crimes Against Humanity: A Historical Perspective* 116 (iUniverse Publishers 2004).

2 Ricci, at 103.

3 Ricci, at 170. Note: all of Ricci's italicized quotes are taken from his book. Ricci died in 2006.

4 Ricci, at 174.

5 Ricci, at 175–76.

6 Ricci, at 177.

7 *Human Warehouse,* HERALD, Oct. 27, 1975.

8 *See Monson Hospital Conditions 'Indefensible,' Says Bellotti.*

9 *Judge Calls Fernald School 'a Pigpen,'* BOS. GLOBE, Feb. 24, 1976.

10 Nils J. Bruzelius, *Judge Tauro Tours 'Nightmare' School,* BOS. GLOBE, at 1.

11 Nils J. Bruzelius, *Judge Tauro Sees Some Progress in Return Trip to Fernald,* BOS. GLOBE.

12 See Nils J. Bruzelius, *Bay State Signs Decrees to Aid Schools for Retarded,* BOS. GLOBE, July 26, 1977; Nils J. Bruzelius, *Millions for Retarded OKd,* BOS. GLOBE, July 25, 1977; Nils J. Bruzelius, *New Hope for 5 State Retarded Schools,* BOS. GLOBE.

13 See Nils J. Bruzelius, *Tauro Tells State It Can't Veto His State-School Plan,* BOS. GLOBE, Dec. 6, 1977; *Buckley Ordered to Outline Belchertown School Progress,* SPRINGFIELD DAILY NEWS, Nov. 11, 1977.

14 Nils J. Bruzelius, *Tauro Sets Deadline for Retarded,* BOS. GLOBE.

15 *See* Walter V. Robinson, *Court Order Snarls Drive to Prorogue,* BOS. GLOBE, July 4, 1980, at 1.

[16] BOS. HERALD, July 5, 1980.

[17] *See* Jean Dietz & William Doherty, *Mental Health Chief Sees Harm in Tauro's Layoff Ban,* BOS. GLOBE, July 29, 1981, at 17.

[18] Sharon Moriearty, *Tauro Ruling Hints of More to Come,* MARC Advoc., Summer 1981.

[19] Robert L. Turner, *Mental Care Funding: Another Collision of the Galaxies?,* BOS. GLOBE.

[20] *See Ricci v. Okin,* 537 F. Supp. 817, 836 (D. Mass. 1982).

[21] *See* Jean Dietz, *Tauro Tells US to Check State Schools,* BOS. GLOBE, May 19, 1983.

[22] *See* Jean Dietz, *Heckler Issues New Warning on Mental Facilities,* BOS. GLOBE, Sept. 10, 1983; Viola Osgood, *Heckler, at Fernald, Threatens Fund Cutoff,* BOS. GLOBE, July 24, 1983.

[23] *Ricci v. Callahan,* 576 F. Supp. 415, 415 (D. Mass. 1983).

[24] *See* Eileen McNamara, *Atkins Agrees to Full Funding at State Schools,* BOS. GLOBE, Dec. 21, 1983, at 1.

CHAPTER 9

The *Rogers* Case

In April 1975, Judge Tauro drew another case that would reshape care in state institutions. Ruby Rogers and six other mentally ill patients committed at Boston State Hospital brought suit against the Commissioner of Mental Health and fourteen other defendants, almost all of them doctors who worked at the hospital. The suit challenged the seclusion and forced medication policies at Boston State, which were similar to policies at other such institutions around the country. Richard Cole, a legal aid attorney, became lead counsel for the plaintiff class, while a battery of private firms and the Attorney General's office represented the defendants. Cole had spearheaded the founding of a legal assistance program at Boston State while he was a third-year student at Boston University School of Law. While talking with patients and staff, Cole learned about disturbing practices at the hospital and, in collaboration with Bob Burdick, who ran the Boston University Clinical program, he tried unsuccessfully to bring an end to them through negotiations with administrators. After graduation, Cole joined the Boston Legal Assistance Project (which later became part of Greater Boston Legal Services), and he got authorization to bring suit.

> *Richard Cole:* When I was out there, I built trust with people. Sometimes I would meet them behind trees and in weird places. They began to tell me about practices that were extremely disturbing to me: holding down patients forcibly, giving them medication against their will, locking patients in seclusion for long periods of time as punishment. We tried to get them to agree to stop these practices, but they felt they needed to continue them.

Plaintiffs' attorneys were pleased to draw Tauro as the judge:

> *Richard Cole:* I went over to file the case in federal court. Steve Baumohl, who was also at Legal Services, came too. When we found out we had drawn Judge Tauro, Steve said "Great!" I had no clue, but Steve had clerked for Judge Tauro a few years earlier, and he felt strongly that Tauro was a person who would be open to understanding the pain that patients were going through, and the significant trauma of being locked up in those smelly, dirty seclusion rooms. The role of the fact finder in a case like that is critical, and we really needed an independent-minded judge who could look at things in a new way, rather than accepting the traditional paternalistic view of mental patients.

Richard Cole

COURTESY OF RICHARD W. COLE

Tauro immediately found himself in the eye of a storm. Plaintiffs moved for a temporary restraining order, seeking to prevent the hospital from confining patients to a seclusion room and from forcing patients to take psychotropic medications over their objections. Plaintiffs' proposed order excepted only emergency situations, specifically and narrowly defined. On April 30, three days after the suit was filed, Judge Tauro granted the restraining order, over defendants' strong objections.

> *Richard Cole:* I had just been sworn in four months before, and here I was arguing before Judge Tauro at the TRO hearing. Steve Baumohl came with me, and he told me: "I am going to put my hand on your leg, and when my hand is on your leg, you keep your mouth shut. Do not get up. When my hand is off your leg, it means yes, you can get up and speak." He was basically saying that there are times when Judge Tauro wants to hear from you, and times when he doesn't, and when he doesn't want to hear from you, you don't want to be saying anything!

The parties agreed to continue the restraining order in effect while they prepared for an extensive hearing on whether or not its terms should be extended in the form of a preliminary injunction. The court heard six days of evidence in the fall, at which point Judge Tauro adjourned the hearing to pursue settlement discussions. Despite extensive negotiations, however, the parties' differences proved irreconcilable, so the court case continued. Defendants filed a motion for summary judgment, which was argued before Tauro in the summer of 1976 and ultimately denied in early 1977. Defendants then brought a motion to dissolve the temporary restraining order, claiming that it had led to a number of instances of violence on the part of unmedicated patients and had adversely impacted conditions in the affected hospital units. When Tauro denied the motion to dissolve, defendants appealed to the First Circuit, where their appeal was denied.

The next step was the trial, which was to be held before Judge Tauro, without a jury, beginning in December 1977.[1] It would prove to be an extraordinarily long and drawn-out affair, with a total of seventy-two trial days spread out over a period of thirteen months. More than fifty witnesses testified, the majority of whom were psychiatrists, psychologists, or other professionals. After trial, both sides filed extensive briefs, and an *amicus* brief was filed by the Massachusetts Psychiatric Society. In all, there were more than 8,000 pages of trial transcript and over 2,300 pages of post-trial briefs and proposed findings.

Judge Tauro was a proactive trial judge, often asking his own questions of witnesses. A *Boston Magazine* article commented:

> [Judge Tauro] frequently intervenes to draw out a witness or to ask clarifying questions of his own. Tauro has made it clear to the attorneys on both sides that he is interested in information, not legal nitpicking, and that he will pursue

A trial exhibit: a seclusion room at Boston State Hospital

COURTESY OF RICHARD W. COLE

> anything a witness says, even a dangling participle that gives cause for curiosity.

At trial, Richard Cole was joined by his former supervisor at the Boston University clinical program, Bob Burdick, and a young lawyer named Clyde Bergstresser. The plan had been to enlist an experienced trial lawyer, Larry Shubow, to join the plaintiffs' trial team, but Shubow was too busy on major litigation involving the Mashpee Indian tribe, so his junior colleague, Clyde Bergstresser, filled in. Bergstresser himself had only a year or so of experience, although he had been in court a good deal more than Cole. It was, as he puts it, "the lame leading the blind."

Both Cole and Bergstresser had moments where they felt that trying a case in front of Judge Tauro, as young attorneys, was like trying a case before their father.

> *Richard Cole:* My father was a very powerful, charismatic man who had a quick temper and was very clear about how he

Artist's rendering of a moment in the Rogers trial. At plaintiffs' counsel table, left to right: Richard Cole, Bob Burdick, and Clyde Bergstresser (standing).

COURTESY OF RICHARD W. COLE

wanted things done. My father and I developed a great relationship after I left the house, but I fought him intensely as a teenager. I felt it was my father's personality I was contending with in the form of Judge Tauro.

Clyde Bergstresser: I grew up in a blue-collar neighborhood in Jersey, where my dad was a beat cop. Judge Tauro was like my dad in some ways. The expression I would use was that you had to pay obeisance to the king. Judge Tauro was in charge of the courtroom, and you needed to recognize that. Things that were disrespectful, like talking when he was talking, you just didn't do. On the other hand, although he would test your mettle, he respected someone who stood up for their position. He wanted you to be assertive, but respectfully assertive. As long as you did that, you were fine. I thought he was a great judge. I consider that I learned how to try in front of him.

Clyde Bergstresser

COURTESY OF CLYDE W. BERGSTRESSER

There was one moment during the trial when Bergstresser got a little carried away, but it worked out fine from his point of view.

Clyde Bergstresser: I was cross-examining one of the defendants and asking him whether it was a departure from good practice to keep a patient locked up in seclusion for 24 hours, or whatever the interval was. It was a lot of hours. The lead attorney on the other side, Steve Schultz, stood up and objected, saying that there wasn't one occasion in which the patient in question had been secluded for more than X hours. I had spent tons and tons of hours going over the records, and at that point I think it was clear I knew the record pretty well. Being a little cocky, I said, "Would Mr. Schultz like to bet the case on that?" At that point, most judges would say: "Mr. Bergstresser, we're not gambling. Move on.", or words to that effect. Instead, Judge Tauro got this big smile and turned to Steve Schultz and said: "Care to take him up on that? We could end this case really fast." Schultz thought about it for a couple of seconds and then sat down.

There was considerable outside attention focused on the case. There had been no prior reported court decisions around the country on the issues raised in the *Rogers* case, and the decision in *Rogers,* as well as that in a pending case in New Jersey that raised similar issues, would likely impact subsequent litigation in other states and the methods of treating committed mental patients around the country. A number of psychiatrists predicted dire consequences if the terms of Judge Tauro's temporary restraining order were perpetuated.

The *Rogers* case was reminiscent of *Ricci* in that it arose in the context of an understaffed institution with substandard facilities. As Judge Tauro found, the Austin Unit, one of the units in question, was "a drab, gloomy, poorly lighted structure in a chronic state of disrepair."[3] The Austin unit also had serious plumbing and heating problems. Conditions at the other unit principally at issue, the May Unit, were similar. The seclusion rooms in particular were "dirty, stark, austere and smelly."[4] Also, as in *Ricci,* there was a plaintiff population unable to care for itself—"victims of fate who ha[d] been shortchanged by life,"[5] as Judge Tauro's opinion would describe them. The result was testimony that was sometimes hard to listen to, such as Rubie Rogers' opening-day testimony that whenever she refused medications she was grabbed by six or seven men and rushed into seclusion and given the needle. She said that because of side effects of the medication she felt "like rats were crawling on my feet and biting them. I didn't sleep...my arms and legs were jerking, twitching uncontrollably.... My whole body quivered."[6] She testified that she had set her hair on fire in an effort to secure her release.

While the plaintiffs' case proceeded there was more testimony in the same vein, such as the testimony of a mental health aide about a woman who would put cigarette butts in her ears or swallow pop tops from soda cans, and testimony that patients were treated like dogs while in seclusion and that three patients had died there. As the litigation was pending, one woman blinded herself with her own hands while in seclusion, causing Judge Tauro to order a probe of what happened.[7]

Rogers differed from *Ricci* in a fundamental way, however: it was a case in which complex, cutting-edge legal issues were at the fore. The *Rogers* defendants had a case on the merits, which they would press passionately. The Austin Unit was affiliated with the Tufts Bay Cove Mental Health Center and served as a teaching facility for Tufts. The May Unit was part of the Solomon Carter Fuller

Mental Health Center and served as a teaching facility for the Boston University Medical School. Most of the defendants were highly credentialed doctors. Most of the plaintiffs, on the other hand, had histories that included episodes of violence, which showed, at least episodically, that they could be a threat to themselves and/or others. One plaintiff, a large and powerful young man with a history of psychosis, had punched an attendant in the chest and threatened people with a rolled coat hanger. Others had assaulted fellow patients. One had set fire to part of a ward. Sometimes the risk of violence was clear, constituting an "emergency" under any definition, and thus the hospital's right to forcibly medicate and/or seclude was uncontested, but other cases were less clear cut. It was a difficult and challenging environment for the doctors, to say the least.

On January 31, 1979, the evidence in the case finally closed. Post-trial briefing followed. Judge Tauro's opinion in the case would come on Halloween of 1979, exactly nine months after the close of evidence. It would be only the second federal district court decision to address the rights of committed mental patients; the other had come just six weeks earlier: the decision of Judge Stanley Brotman in the New Jersey case of *Rennie v. Klein*.[8] *Rennie* was a decision on a preliminary injunction, which followed a total of thirty-one days of hearings, fourteen of them when Rennie was the only plaintiff and seventeen more after the case had been certified as a class action. Judge Brotman held that both voluntary and involuntary patients at mental hospitals have a qualified constitutional right to refuse treatment and a right to due process before drugs can be forcibly administered. Against a factual background of what Judge Brotman found to be widespread, improper practices, including over-reliance on psychotropic medications and inadequate attention to patients' objections to being medicated and to side effects of the medications, the court ruled that voluntarily committed patients had an absolute right to refuse medication in non-emergency situations, and that involuntarily committed patients had a similar right, except that it could be overridden in cases where a neutral independent decision-maker supported the decision to medicate. The independent neutral could be a staff physician, but not one who was a member of the patient's treatment team. The court did not require either a formal hearing or the presence of a lawyer.

Judge Tauro's opinion in the *Rogers* case would be a second major court victory for mental patients, but his analysis and remedy differed from that of the New Jersey court in important ways. Tauro did not ground his ruling on any findings of improper practices on the part of defendants; in fact, he found that they had acted in good faith and that their actions were consistent with accepted medical practice. Nevertheless, Tauro found that committed mental patients had rights under Massachusetts law, and under the U.S. Constitution, which allowed them to refuse treatment and avoid seclusion, except in cases of emergency. He defined emergency situations as those in which "a failure [to medicate] would result in a substantial likelihood of physical harm to that patient, other patients, or to staff members of the institution."[9] Judge Tauro invoked the First Amendment as one basis for his opinion, noting that psychotropic medications are mind-altering. He wrote:

> Whatever powers the Constitution has granted our government, involuntary mind control is not one of them, absent extraordinary circumstances. The fact that mind control takes place in a mental institution in the form of medically sound treatment of mental disease is not, in itself, an extraordinary circumstance warranting an unsanctioned intrusion on the integrity of a human being.[10]

In cases of committed mental patients, Tauro held that a guardian must be appointed to manage the patient's affairs, with the role of the guardian being to act consistently with the patient's wishes, as opposed to making his or her own judgment as to what is in the patient's best interests. In the event of a dispute, the matter would be resolved by the court, after a formal hearing. Tauro rejected the defendants' central argument that the judgments of lawyers and the judicial process should not be substituted for medical judgments in such cases. He wrote:

> One basic theme that seems to thread its way through most of defendants' arguments is that a federal court has no business second-guessing a treatment decision of a hospital staff person. This contention is like saying that once there is confinement in prison there can be no judicial scrutiny as to the conditions of confinement. As Chief Judge Bazelon in the D.C. Circuit put it:
>
> > "It makes little sense to guard zealously against the possibility of unwarranted deprivations prior to hospitalization, only to abandon the watch once the patient disappears behind hospital doors."

> Professional judgments concerning confined persons, whether they be made by wardens or physicians in hospitals, should always be subject to judicial scrutiny, given an allegation of constitutional deprivation. Such an allegation has been made here, and it is well founded.[11]

Judge Tauro was not persuaded by the defendants' argument that their options to use forced medication and seclusion in certain non-emergency situations were essential to their ability to treat patients effectively and to maintain a secure environment.

> The defendants' crystal ball foretells a tale of gloom if the standards imposed by this court's temporary restraining order (TRO) are made permanent. But, their prediction is not borne out by the experience of that order.... Dr. Gill...could identify only 12 patients out of 1,000 who refused their medication for prolonged periods...and most of those changed their minds within a few days. None of these patients was transferred to a more secure institutional setting because of behavior problems.
>
> In at least one instance of violence by a patient who refused treatment, Dr. Gill acknowledged at trial that the signs of likely physical harm, absent forced medication, were present and the consequences predictable. Forced medication would, therefore, have been permissible under the provisions of the TRO. The subsequent violence in that situation was, therefore, not a function of the TRO, but was due to the staff's failure to act in accordance with its professional judgment. Doctors, like judges, are in a decision making profession. Some decisions are clear and others less certain. Neither profession has room for those unwilling or unable to make the tough ones.[12]

Besides their request for injunctive relief, plaintiffs also sought money damages. On this, Judge Tauro ruled for the defendants, finding that their actions had been taken in "good faith" and consistently with accepted medical practice. Judge Tauro explained this decision in part by reference to the conditions under which the defendants worked.

> Of significance to this court...are the less than desirable conditions in which defendants were required to deal with plaintiffs. The facilities and support staff at Boston State were marginal, at best. In contrast, the patient population was extremely demanding, both in terms of numbers and their potential for disruptive behavior. Defendants did not have the luxury of detached, leisurely reflection as they faced the innumerable crises that characterized daily living on the Austin and May wards.... To hold them liable in damages, given the totality of the circumstances presented by the evidence in this case, would be unfair to them and contrary to the public interest.[13]

The *Rogers* decision was reported in the Boston papers,[14] *The New York Times*[15] and the *National Law Journal,*[16] among others. Plaintiffs' counsel Richard Cole commented that the protections for committed mental patients under the *Rogers* decision went far beyond those provided by the New Jersey court in the *Rennie* case. The *Boston Globe* published an editorial in support.[17]

Not everyone, of course, was happy about the decision. One of those who blasted the decision was Harvard psychologist Alan Stone, president of the American Psychiatric Association. Stone was quoted as saying that Judge Tauro's decision in *Rogers* was "the most impossible, inappropriate, ill-considered decision ever made in the field of mental health law."[18]

Around the same time, newspapers carried the story of a paranoid schizophrenic former patient at Boston State Hospital who had refused to take his shots and then attacked his father. The altercation resulted in one policeman being seriously injured and the patient himself being in poor condition after being shot by the police. The patient's mother blamed Judge Tauro's decision in *Rogers,* saying: "I am extremely critical of the judge.... My son was no dummy. [He] was aware of this law."[19]

The *Rogers* Appeals

Judge Tauro's decision was not the last word in the case. The defendants appealed to the First Circuit, accepting the restrictions the decision had placed on their use of segregation units, but challenging the restrictions on their use of forced medications. The plaintiffs, in turn, cross-appealed, challenging the denial of their claim for money damages.

The First Circuit opinion, when it came in November 1980, was more sympathetic to defendants' arguments than Tauro's opinion had been. The court's analysis began by agreeing with Judge Tauro's conclusion that committed mental patients were presumed competent to make medical decisions for themselves, unless and until they were adjudicated incompetent to do so. The court also agreed that they had a liberty interest protected under both Massachusetts law and the U.S. Constitution to be free from unwanted medication. The Court of Appeals parted company from Judge Tauro, however, in its view of how to weigh the state's competing interest in managing the institution and avoiding violence and in its approach to how differences in assessing these interests should be resolved. As a predicate to its approach, the First Circuit noted a disagreement with the trial court on one aspect of the evidence.

> To a certain extent it is clear that throughout this litigation defendants and their supporting amici have erroneously attributed acts of violence to the strictness of the court's standard. Nevertheless, it does appear that the district court may have overlooked or misconstrued evidence of specific acts of violence occurring as a result of defendants' difficulty in applying the court's standard.[20]

The Court of Appeals criticized the standard for "emergency" employed by Judge Tauro as overly restrictive, saying that it could be interpreted as allowing forced medication only when violence was "more likely than not," which would potentially prevent its use in instances where there was a risk of serious violence, or even death, but in which the probability of that happening was under fifty percent.

The second major difference between the approach of Judge Tauro and that of the Court of Appeals was perhaps more fundamental. The Court of Appeals accepted the defendants' principal argument that the court should not put itself in the business of second guessing doctors on complicated treatment issues. Accordingly, the court held that the balancing of the patients' interests with those of the state in preventing violence should be left to an independent physician.

> [T]he court should leave this difficult, necessarily ad hoc balancing to state physicians and limit its own role to designing procedures for ensuring that the patients' interests in refusing antipsychotics are taken into consideration and that antipsychotics are not forcibly administered absent a finding by a qualified physician that those interests are outweighed in a particular situation and less restrictive alternatives are unavailable.[21]

Appeals again followed, and the U.S. Supreme Court agreed to hear the case,[22] which was not surprising given its importance and the undeveloped state of the law in the area. Before the case got to oral argument, however, another case intervened. While the *Rogers* case had been pending in the Massachusetts federal court, there was a parallel case working its way through the Massachusetts state courts, which raised the question of whether a *non-institutionalized* mentally incompetent person had the right to refuse treatment with antipsychotic drugs. That case worked its way up to the Supreme Judicial Court (SJC) of Massachusetts, and in early 1981 the SJC issued its opinion, ruling in favor of the plaintiff.[23] The SJC held that a person did not lose his or her liberty interest in not having unwanted medication by virtue of becoming incompetent, but rather that in such cases that person's interests should be represented by a guardian, and it would be up to a court to determine what the incompetent patient would have wanted—a so-called "substituted judgment" determination.[24]

Because the Massachusetts court was the ultimate authority on Massachusetts law, and because it was quite possible that the plaintiffs in the *Rogers* case might have rights under Massachusetts law more extensive than their rights under federal law, the U.S. Supreme Court recognized that the opinion in *In re Guardianship of Roe* had potentially decisive implications for the *Rogers* case. Consequently, the Supreme Court decided the better course would be to send the case back to the Court of Appeals, with instructions for it to seek guidance from the SJC on the issues of Massachusetts law raised in *Rogers.*[25] The First Circuit, in turn, followed that mandate, framing nine questions which it sent to the SJC.[26]

The SJC's unanimous opinion, written by Justice Ruth Abrams and issued in November 1983, came to much the same conclusion as had Judge Tauro four years earlier: the involuntary commitment of a mental patient is not a determination of incompetency; competency has to be determined in a court proceeding; and no state interest is sufficiently compelling in a non-emergency situation to overcome a decision of an incompetent mental patient to refuse treatment by antipsychotic drugs. As it had in *Guardianship of Roe,* the court held that the applicable standard in proceedings relating to incompetent patients was the "substituted judgment" standard, namely, what would the patient want to do if he or she were in a position to speak for himself? If the patient objected to being medicated in a non-emergency situation, the guardian was required to go to court to obtain a ruling under the substituted judgment rule before forced medication would be allowed.[27]

Following the SJC's opinion, the First Circuit remanded the *Rogers* case to the trial court for proceedings consistent with the SJC opinion and the case finally concluded. Today, pursuant to the SJC's decision, and to Judge Tauro's original opinion in *Rogers,* a "Rogers order"—a court ruling under the substituted judgment standard permitting forced medication—has become a familiar part of the lexicon in institutions for mental patients in Massachusetts and now in many other states as well. At the same time, the use of seclusion and the use of forced medication have become far less common.

Roderick MacLeish, Jr., was a clerk to Judge Tauro, and was assigned to work on the *Rogers* case. MacLeish has gone on to spend much of his career representing the disabled and their family members, and has received awards from the Alliance for the Mentally Ill of Massachusetts and the Coalition of Families and Advocates for the Retarded.

In 2009, Ruby Rogers died.

Roderick MacLeish, Jr.

COURTESY OF HON. JOSEPH L. TAURO

Richard Cole: When you think about the lawsuit and the impact of Judge Tauro's decision, it is striking. You use the term "Rogers orders" and everyone knows what they are.

There is a Ruby Rogers Center. When she died, the Department of Mental Health had an event to celebrate her life. Her family came up from Virginia. I was invited and went. It was phenomenal to talk to the family about Ruby. But

Front of the program for the celebration of Ruby Rogers' life, sponsored by the Department of Mental Health

DIGITAL IMAGE OF PROGRAM COVER COURTESY OF RICHARD W. COLE

what was most remarkable was the total change of mentality around the issues of medication and getting patients on board. Ruby is remembered in such a powerful way by people who never met her, but who struggled with mental health issues. She is a model for them—an example that you can do something meaningful in your life even though day by day it may be difficult and painful for you to get through a day.

NOTES

1 Nils Bruzelius, *Patient Rights Trial Opens in US Court,* BOS. GLOBE, Dec. 9, 1977.

2 Susan Quinn, *Mass. Insanity: Is Madness a Disease, or a Person's Constitutional Right?,* BOS. MAG., Jan. 9, 1978, at 75, 76, 121.

3 *Rogers v. Okin,* 478 F. Supp. 1342, 1356 (D. Mass. 1979).

4 *Id.* at 1373.

5 *Id.* at 1369.

6 Nils J. Bruzelius, *Patient Set Six Fires, Court Told,* BOS. GLOBE, Mar. 23, 1978, at 48.

7 *See* Nils J. Bruzelius, *She Blinded Herself with Her Own Hands,* BOS. GLOBE, Mar. 8, 1979.

8 462 F. Supp. 1131 (D.N.J. 1979).

9 *Rogers,* 478 F. Supp. at 1365.

10 *Id.*

11 *Id.* at 1371 (quoting *Covington v. Harris,* 419 F.2d 617, 623–24 (D.C. Cir. 1969)).

12 *Id.* at 1369 & n.36.

13 *Id.* at 1383.

14 *See, e.g.,* Nils J. Bruzelius, *Mental Patients Win Rights,* BOS. GLOBE, Oct. 30, 1979.

[15] *See Judge Curbs Forced Medication in Treatment of Mental Patients,* N.Y. TIMES, Nov. 1, 1979.

[16] *See* Edward J. Burke, *Judge: 1st Amendment 'Right to Think' Lets Mental Patients Refuse Medication,* NAT'L L.J., Nov. 12, 1979.

[17] *See* Editorial, *A Clear Course for Mental Health,* BOS. GLOBE, Nov. 4, 1979, at A4.

[18] *See* Edward J. Burke, *Judge: 1st Amendment 'Right to Think' Lets Mental Patients Refuse Medication,* NAT'L L.J., Nov. 12, 1979.

[19] Earl Marchand, *Refusal to Take Drug Leads to a Tragedy,* BOS. HERALD AM., Nov. 17, 1979, at A4.

[20] *Rogers v. Okin,* 634 F.2d 650, 655 (1st Cir. 1980).

[21] *Id.* at 657.

[22] *Okin v. Rogers,* 451 U.S. 906 (1981).

[23] *See In re Guardianship of Roe,* 383 Mass. 415 (1981).

[24] *Id.* at 434.

[25] *See Mills v. Rogers,* 457 U.S. 291 (1982).

[26] *See Rogers v. Comm'r of the Dep't of Mental Health,* 390 Mass. 489, 490 (1983).

[27] *See id.* at 500.

CHAPTER 10

Litigation: Politics, Race, Equal Protection, and the First Amendment

Drinan v. Nixon and *Doe v. Bush*

Another high-profile case that came before Judge Tauro early in his federal court career pitted a group of congressmen, angry about U.S. bombing in Cambodia, against President Richard Nixon. The lead plaintiff was Father Robert Drinan, a Roman Catholic priest and a liberal Massachusetts Congressman who had been an outspoken critic of the Vietnam War. *Drinan v. Nixon* was filed in mid-1973, after the end of the Vietnam War. The last of the U.S. ground forces had withdrawn from Vietnam in the summer of 1972, and the war ended formally with the signing of the Paris Peace Accords on January 27, 1973, just after Judge Tauro went on the bench. There was still a civil war ongoing in Cambodia, however, in which the United States had intervened, conducting a bombing campaign on behalf of the incumbent leader Lon Nol in his fight with the deposed Prince Sihanouk and Sihanouk's communist allies. Anger at the earlier American invasion of Cambodia in 1970, which had been an attempt to shut off infiltration routes to South Vietnam used by the North Vietnamese, had been a major factor motivating Father Drinan to run for Congress in the first place.

The 1973 Cambodian bombing campaign made Drinan even angrier than the earlier bombing of Cambodia had, and he had plenty of company. Congress passed a resolution outlawing the bombing; President Nixon immediately vetoed the resolution. Father Drinan then introduced the first resolution calling for the impeachment of the President, on the basis that Nixon's unauthorized conduct of the war in Cambodia constituted "high crimes and misdemeanors" impeachable under the Constitution. At the same time, Drinan and three other Massachusetts congressmen brought suit in Massachusetts federal court seeking to enjoin the bombing in Cambodia, which they argued was in violation of domestic and international law. They contended that any arguable congressional authorization for American military action in Cambodia had expired on the signing of the Paris Peace Accords and the return of American prisoners of war by the North Vietnamese.

While Drinan's case was pending before Judge Tauro, the political battles continued to rage in Washington. On June 30, 1973 a compromise between the Nixon administration and the Congress was announced: President Nixon committed to end the bombing of Cambodia on or before August 15, 1973, and not to undertake military action in Cambodia after that date without first seeking congressional approval. In the meantime, Congress would sit tight.

The June 30 compromise did not moot *Drinan v. Nixon,* since Drinan and his co-plaintiffs were not party to the compromise. They pressed their position in court that the war was illegal, and the government moved to dismiss the suit. On August 8, just a week before the bombing was scheduled to end under the compromise agreement, Tauro handed down his decision ordering the case dismissed. Tauro held that the dispute presented a "political question" which under the law was within the responsibility of the legislative and executive branches, not the judiciary.[1] Tauro's opinion suggested that there might have been a basis for the court to get involved if there had been a dispute between the legislative and executive branches presenting a question of their respective authority, but in light of the June 30 compromise, the branches were in agreement and the court should stand aside.

> *Joe Tauro:* My law clerk working on that case was Mark Brodin, a good guy who is now a professor at Boston College Law School. I told him how I wanted the case to come out and asked him to draft a short opinion. He gave me an atrocious draft. He didn't want the case to come out that way, he wanted me to enjoin the bombing. I was letting him down. He's a young man and I'm no longer young and I'm not thinking the same way that he's thinking.

I can see him standing across from me saying: "Well, Judge, I did the best I could." I said: "OK, don't you worry about it. I'll take care of it."

And I did. I went off and wrote a very short opinion, by hand, and I handed it to Mark and asked him to type it up. He took it and then he later told me that he wanted to take a shot at smoothing it over, or something along those lines. He recognized his responsibility, and he dug into my draft to make it better and I'm sure he did make it better. Your law clerks can get emotional, and this was a very emotional issue, but it was the only time in 37 years that I can remember someone abdicating a bit, until he rallied.

One thing that was gratifying about the case was that we were cited and discussed by the Second Circuit Court of Appeals when it ruled the same way on a similar case shortly after ours. I think it was Congresswoman Bella Abzug and maybe some others who had brought suit down there.

Mark Brodin: It was a rough time in my clerkship. I felt very strongly that the bombing of Cambodia was immoral and wrong-headed. For me it was a transcendent issue. The judge made it clear what his view was of the law and how the case should come out, but I found it very hard to be the clerk working on the opinion that was going to throw out Father Drinan's suit.

Mark Brodin, three decades later as a Boston College law professor

COURTESY OF MARK BRODIN

After I passed in what I think was the second draft, the judge said to me: "Mark, I think you're having real difficulty with this." He suggested that I take a week off to think about things. To his credit, he was able to understand my position and not view it as a sign of disloyalty. I went camping with my girlfriend, and when I came back I did what I could to help out.

Thirty years later, Judge Tauro had a similar case and came to the same conclusion. In *Doe I v. Bush,*[2] plaintiffs were members of the military, parents of military personnel, and members of the House of Representatives opposed to the impending war in Iraq. The congressional plaintiffs were some of the "who's who" of the liberal wing of the House: John Conyers, Dennis Kucinich, Jesse Jackson, Jr., Jim McDermott, Jose Serrano, and Sheila Jackson Lee. Proclaiming that "the President is not a king," plaintiffs sought a preliminary injunction to prevent President Bush and Secretary of Defense Donald Rumsfeld from ordering the invasion of Iraq. As in the *Drinan* case, the central argument was that the executive lacked the authority to declare and prosecute a war without a declaration of war by the Congress. Tauro again found that the case raised a "political question" that should be left to the other branches of government to resolve.[3] As in the *Drinan* case, Tauro's opinion noted that if Congress and the executive had been "clearly and resolutely in opposition" over the conduct of the war, raising an "intractable constitutional gridlock," the matter would have been up to the court, but that was not the case. Congress had not collectively opposed the war; on the contrary, it had passed a resolution months earlier that offered support for the executive's position.

In the end, Brodin and Tauro forged a strong relationship which has remained close ever since. Now when they get together they can reminisce about the bumpy spots, like the tension over the Drinan opinion, or the period when both were new to their jobs.

> *Mark Brodin:* I was his first clerk, and it was a very daunting job at first. Then very early on, I came down with a severe intestinal condition and had to be taken to the MGH where they told me I had salmonella. I called the office to say I wouldn't be coming in, and I spoke to Judge Tauro's secretary at the time, Mary Coughlin, who everybody called "Chickie." She told me: "You don't have salmonella, you have Tauroitis. It's rough at first."

The At-Large Voting Challenge

Two years after the *Drinan* case, Judge Tauro drew another high-profile case which raised questions about the prerogatives of the legislative branch and the role of judiciary. The plaintiffs in *Black Voters v. McDonough*[4] challenged the "at-large" method of electing the Boston School Committee. For years the six-member committee had been all white, whereas by the 1970s the majority of the students in Boston's public schools were non-white. Plaintiffs claimed that in light of the fact that most Boston voters were white and that most white Boston voters tended to vote for white candidates over black candidates, at-large voting prejudiced the chances of black candidates to win. They argued that a district-based voting system should be used instead.

When the *Black Voters* case went to trial before Judge Tauro without a jury in the spring of 1976, racial tensions in the city were high. Just two years earlier, in June 1974, Judge Arthur Garrity had issued his opinion in the Boston school desegregation case, and when the school committee failed to present an adequate desegregation plan to the court by the following January, the court had taken on the role of overseeing implementation of its desegregation order.

At the heart of the court's desegregation plan was forced busing, a practice that many in some of Boston's white neighborhoods railed against passionately. Some of the defendants in the *Black Voters* case were representative public officials who had become heroes to many of their constituents for their vocal opposition to busing and their defiance of the federal court, like school committee member Elvira "Pixie" Palladino, and city councilors Louise Day Hicks and John Kerrigan. Tauro's courtroom was packed for the thirty days of trial, in which thirty-two witnesses testified. Newspaper coverage was heavy.

Tauro's decision in October 1976 upheld the at-large voting system. The opinion reviewed the results of various elections over the prior fifteen or so years, including the two-time election of Tom Atkins, a black candidate, to the city council under an at-large voting system, and elections in which Ed Brooke, also a black candidate, had carried Boston in state-wide elections for Massachusetts Attorney General, as well as elections in which black candidates had placed seventh in the voting for school committee and therefore just missed election.

Tauro recognized that high feelings over busing had exacerbated tendencies to vote along racial lines, but he did not expect things necessarily to remain at a fever pitch.

> The court is not equipped with a crystal ball to predict the future. But, if history is any guide, as the seasons change so will the controlling political issues. It is now clear, if it has not been in the past, that court-ordered busing in Boston is constitutional, and will continue until its purpose is achieved.

> It will soon become apparent to the public, if it is not already, that the School Committee has no power to resist the federal court busing order, regardless of political rhetoric to the contrary. As the public becomes mindful that this is so, strident and uncompromising opposition to the orders of this court will undoubtedly shrink in importance as a qualification for election.[5]

Tauro did not see the problem of lack of success of black candidates the same way the plaintiffs did.

> *Joe Tauro:* The plaintiffs blamed the lack of success of black candidates on the districting, but they didn't register enough voters. You couldn't blame it on the system, you needed to get out the voters— then they would have a chance.

In the end, despite finding that voting patterns were to some extent racially polarized, Tauro did not find that plaintiffs had proved a violation of their constitutional rights or of the Voting Rights Act, so he let the at-large system stand.

> The at-large system has been in effect for a century. It was not instituted as a means for diluting black voting power. Although, in its present form, there is serious question as to whether it is the best system available, there is a rational theory for its use in Boston's School Committee elections. The responsibility for providing quality education for all Boston's school children is a universal, city-wide problem. Those elected should have the well-being of the entire population in mind as they make their decisions. The fact that some may not have lived up to this responsibility may be good cause for removing them from office, but their failure is not adequate cause to suspend the Charter of the City of Boston.[6]

Although neither of them were there during the trial, John Nadas and Ellen Gesmer were Tauro's law clerks at the time the decision in the *Black Voters* case was rendered. It was Nadas who left his mark on the opinion, literally.

> *John Nadas:* This was long before word processors or any of the technical capabilities we have now. The judge had decided that the opinion was going to be issued on a certain day, and Ellen Gesmer and I were given the job of proofreading the opinion and checking everything over the night before to make sure that that the opinion, which was a long one, was in perfect shape to be issued first thing the next morning. While we were doing this, I managed to knock a cup of coffee over on the opinion. Ellen and I locked the door and wouldn't let the judge in while we set about madly drying the opinion off with a paper towel and then hanging each page out to dry by means of paper clips. The opinion went out the next morning.

John Nadas. Nadas for many years has been the co-managing partner of Choate LLP in Boston.

COURTESY OF JOHN NADAS

Tauro later called his decision in the *Black Voters* case the toughest he had made. The decision in *Black Voters* was hailed by some of the whites who had been fanning the flames of racial discord and was loudly criticized by many in the black community. It was an uncomfortable position for Tauro, but vindication was not long in coming. Four weeks after Tauro's decision, Boston voters again went to the polls to vote for school committee. This time, John O'Bryant, a black candidate who had been narrowly defeated in an earlier election, was successful. One newspaper column commented:

> Thus it appears that the Tauro formula has worked. Boston will have far more representative governing bodies than would have been the case it the court had acted...what Tauro recognized...is that in a city's political life, unlike its school system, responsive and representative government must be achieved by its citizens.

Ironically, frustration at Tauro's decision was credited by many as having played a key role in O'Bryant's victory by helping to motivate the increased registration of black voters which the decision itself had noted as key to the victory of black candidates.

Further vindication for the decision in the case came a few years later, as Judge Tauro's law clerk on the case and current colleague on the Massachusetts federal court, Michael Ponsor, recalls.

> *Michael Ponsor:* I think it was about three or four years afterward that the people of Boston voted to change the system to a district-based system. Feelings in Boston were still very high in the wake of the federal court's decision taking over the schools. Thus, to have a federal judge come in at that point and cram a new voting system down peoples' throats would have added to the venomous atmosphere and been much less effective than allowing things to go along and the people then changing it themselves by plebiscite, as it happened.
>
> That was a very difficult case, but the evidence that there had been attractive minority candidates thwarted by a white voting bloc was thin; there actually had been some amount of success by minority candidates. It was a case where the judge was really doing some judging.

Housing Discrimination in Boston

A little over ten years later, Judge Tauro drew another important case involving race discrimination in Boston, *NAACP v. Boston Housing Authority.* A Housing and Urban Affairs report from the mid 1980s found systematic discrimination in Boston's public housing practices. Minority applications to certain predominantly white housing projects were regularly denied. The resulting lawsuit brought by the NAACP was hard fought, with bitter feelings and regular leaks to the press as both sides aired their grievances. Tauro did not relish trying the case, with the inflammation of bad feelings across the city that would inevitably result. He pushed hard to get the parties to settle the case. It was a long process, at the brink of

Barbara Arnwine

COURTESY OF BARBARA ARNWINE

failure many times. Plaintiffs' attorney Barbara Arnwine of the Lawyers' Committee for Civil Rights Under Law recalls:

> *Barbara Arnwine:* I remember storming out of one meeting, telling the city lawyers: "You need to learn some new language." There were many times that I was so angry I could have thrown things at people. Bad blood flowed often.

When negotiations stalled, Tauro would intervene.

> *Diane Wilkerson:* Too many times communication totally broke down. Judge Tauro would step in. His primary influence was reminding people what it would take to try the case.

> *Joe Tauro:* It was an exercise in persuasion, in bringing people together. At the time we were just a hair's breadth from having an explosive situation in the City of Boston. There was a lot of temper. In that kind of situation you need to get some of the heat out. Give people a chance to vent. Then the steam goes out, and you can start talking about what ought to be done.

The city and the Boston Housing Authority (BHA) were willing to agree to change their practices going forward, but the big stumbling block was monetary damages, which the plaintiffs were insisting on and which the city was resisting. In the end, plaintiffs prevailed on that point, and an award averaging around \$2,500 for each affected family—a total of around \$3 million—was included in the settlement. The case was settled in October 1989. In his order approving the settlement, Judge Tauro acknowledged the "tough and often confrontational working sessions," but he lauded the perseverance of the parties and what he called "an unstated determination on the part of everyone in the room that Boston would not become another Yonkers."[7] A *Boston Globe* editorial praised Tauro's role in resolving the case: "For Tauro, who brokered the settlement, it was a victory for judicial activism on one of the most vexing issues facing the federal judiciary. A settlement avoided a divisive trial that could have engaged the judge's energies for years."[8]

Boston Mayor Ray Flynn, Judge Tauro, and NAACP President Benjamin Hooks, after signing the consent decree in NAACP v. Boston Housing Authority *in October 1989.*

COURTESY OF HON. JOSEPH L. TAURO

Tauro worked with the lawyers in the BHA settlement case, but he also worked with their clients:

> *Joe Tauro:* Benjamin Hooks was calling the shots for the BHA, and Mayor Flynn was calling them for the city. They were both reasonable guys, and I would talk with them. I've done that several times.
>
> Mayor Menino, the current mayor, is another guy I have worked with and one who is very cooperative. I remember one case where a woman had been badly hurt and was suing the city. I told Menino that I thought he should pay a million dollars to settle the case, but I also told him that if he agreed to do that, I would never come back to him for a nickel more. He agreed to pay the money. I had some credibility with him, and he knew I would keep my word. The case settled.

The Boston Latin Case

It was a very different landscape, politically and legally, when Judge Tauro drew another closely watched case raising sensitive issues of race in Boston's public schools in the late 1990s. *Wessmann v. Boston School Committee*[9] involved a challenge to the admissions policies of one of Boston's elite public high schools, Boston Latin School, which gave a preference to minority candidates for some spots in its incoming class based on a complicated formula intended to promote diversity.

The suit was a successor to a prior suit that forced the school committee to abandon a quota system boosting minority admissions at Latin. In that case, the federal court granted a preliminary injunction in favor of the white plaintiff, who was then admitted. Judge Arthur Garrity, who had presided over the Boston school desegregation case—which, among other things, forced the desegregation of Boston Latin—was the one who allowed the preliminary injunction. In doing so, he commented that it was possible that a different, non-quota-based admissions system intended to promote diversity might survive a court challenge.

Judge Arthur Garrity

COURTESY OF THE U.S. DISTRICT COURT FOR THE DISTRICT OF MASSACHUSETTS

The school committee got Judge Garrity's message. It set up a blue-ribbon panel, assisted *pro bono* by Bain Consulting, which led to the adoption of a new admissions policy at Latin. Under the new policy, half the incoming class was admitted strictly on the basis of test scores and grades, while the second half was admitted partially on the basis of test scores and grades, but with the proviso that the percentages of those of different racial groups admitted to fill these spots should reflect the percentages of those groups represented in the qualified applicant pool. The plaintiff in the case before Judge Tauro, Sarah Wessmann, was one of eleven white students not admitted but who would have been admitted had the admissions system been entirely race blind.

Ever since the Supreme Court's split decision in 1978's *Regents of the University of California v. Bakke,* the courts had wrestled with the question of whether and to what extent racial preferences favoring minority groups were constitutional. By the time the *Wessmann* case went to trial in 1998, the prevailing trend was decidedly against minority preferences in school admissions. In an important 1996 case, *Hopwood v. State of Texas,*[10] the Fifth Circuit Court of Appeals found the University of Texas' law school admissions policy unconstitutional, holding that the state's desire to promote diversity at a law school was not compelling and thus the minority preference could not be sustained. The *Hopwood* decision, rendered from another circuit, was not binding on Judge Tauro, but it was a decision the Supreme Court had let stand, and it was relied on heavily by Wessmann's attorneys in their argument.

Wessmann went to trial beginning in late January 1998. Following thirteen days of trial, and review of extensive post-trial briefs, Tauro ruled for the defendants, upholding the admissions policy. Knowing that an appeal would come and that there was a serious risk of reversal, Tauro wrote a careful opinion which justified the admissions policy as narrowly tailored to serve the state's compelling interest in diversity in its secondary schools:

> More than any other public institution, the public secondary schools awaken our children to cultural values and practices of civility that lead to tolerance and understanding of divergent political, religious and social convictions...
>
> Of great significance is the fact that diversity in the classroom is the most effective of all weapons in challenging stereotypical preconceptions. When studying side by side, in a diverse setting, students grow to understand and respect the differences among them as they share life in a complex, pluralistic society. And, as important, they learn that most people, regardless of their backgrounds, think in fundamentally the same way about matters of character, team work and mutual respect.[11]

Ultimately, Tauro's opinion was in vain, as were the efforts of the school committee to devise an admissions policy that promoted racial diversity at Boston Latin. A panel of the First Circuit voted two to one to reverse the decision, finding the policy to constitute an unconstitutional racial preference.[12] The concurring opinion of Judge Boudin called the Boston Latin admissions policy "a thoughtful effort to assist minorities historically disadvantaged while, at the same time, preserving the essentially competitive character of the schools in question."[13] Nevertheless, he concluded that the Supreme Court precedents did not allow for such a policy without strong evidence establishing that a certain level of minority enrollment was necessary to promote diversity of views and backgrounds, or else establishing that the racial preference in the admissions system was narrowly tailored to meet specifically demonstrated discrimination. The defendants' petition to the U. S. Supreme Court for *certiorari* was denied.

> *Joe Tauro:* I thought the plan that Boston Latin came up with was ingenious, and I felt it was constitutional. I wrote what I thought was a very good opinion, but I couldn't get it to stick. I think in the end there were three votes for cert on the Supreme Court.

Tauro's opinion in the Boston Latin case did not carry the day, but it had plenty of supporters. One First Circuit judge who did not sit on the panel, Hugh Bownes, later wrote in a letter to Tauro that he felt Tauro had decided the case correctly, and regretted that he had not been on the panel to hear the appeal. Tony Lewis of the *New York Times* put his support to Tauro a little more colorfully:

> *Anthony Lewis:* Comparing your opinion to the First Circuit's makes me think of Hamlet showing his mother the portraits of his father and his uncle: "Look here, upon this picture, and on this.... Here is your husband, like a mildew'd ear, blasting his brother."

The Veterans' Preference Litigation

In the mid-1970s a group of women brought a suit challenging the constitutionality of the Massachusetts statute granting veterans an absolute preference in state civil service hiring. Virtually every state in the union had a statute granting some sort of advantage to veterans in civil service hiring, typically in the form of an award of extra points giving veterans an edge in point-based hiring systems, or else in the form of a tie-breaker, whereby veterans were hired ahead of equally qualified non-veterans. Massachusetts was one of five states with a much stronger veterans' preference statute, which provided that all veterans applying for civil service positions went on a hiring list ahead of all non-veterans, regardless of scores on the civil service examination. The result of the statute was the total preclusion of non-veterans from the most sought-after civil service appointments.

The case, *Feeney v. Commonwealth of Massachusetts,*[14] was heard by a three-judge panel of the District Court. The panel included Judge Tauro, his good friend and District Court colleague Frank Murray, and Judge Levin Campbell of the First Circuit. Both sides were well represented: for the plaintiffs were Tom Dignan of Ropes & Gray and John Reinstein of the Civil Liberties Union; representing the defendants was Tom Kiley, First Assistant Attorney General, with John Curtin of Bingham, Dana & Gould submitting an *amicus curiae* brief on behalf of the American Legion.

The plaintiffs acknowledged that aiding veterans was a legitimate and laudable goal, and that the statute did not expressly discriminate against women. It did have a dramatically disparate impact on women, however. Standards for hiring women in the armed services were much stricter than for men: women needed higher test scores, they needed to be in better physical condition, and their eligible age was higher, among other things. Also, the hiring of women was capped at no more than two percent of the Army. Accordingly, the absolute preference for veterans in choice civil service hiring effectively blocked out of these positions for all but the few women veterans. The defense acknowledged these facts, but argued that it was not just females but all non-veterans, most of whom were male, who were being kept out of these jobs, and that statutes favoring veterans were long-standing, widespread, and legal.

In March 1976, the court ruled two to one for the plaintiffs, with Judge Tauro writing the opinion of the court. Judge Campbell concurred and Judge Murray dissented. Judge Tauro wrote:

> Clearly, the rewarding of those who have rendered public service as members of the military is a worthy state purpose. But, equally as clear is that the means employed by the Commonwealth for achieving that purpose, the preference formula, succeeds at the absolute and permanent disadvantage of another clearly identifiable group, Massachusetts' women.
>
> The pivotal question before us, therefore, is, given the legitimate state purpose of assisting veterans, does the means by which Massachusetts implements that purpose in the area

> of public employment unconstitutionally deprive women of their equal protection rights under the Fourteenth Amendment. Our answer is that it does and, therefore, that ch. 31, § 23 is unconstitutional.[15]
>
> ...[T]his Veterans' Preference formula, tied as it is to federal military enrollment policy, is neither fair nor equitable in its impact on women.[16]

Douglas Woodlock, now a colleague of Tauro on the Massachusetts federal court, clerked for Judge Murray on the case.

> *Doug Woodlock:* It was an interesting panel, with Campbell and Tauro, two Massachusetts liberal Republicans, and Frank Murray, a Harry Truman kind of Democrat. It was at the cutting edge of what was happening in equal protection law. Murray drew the line. He usually was not a dissenter but he would not go along.

For a while, it looked like there might be no appeal by the Commonwealth. The state officers against whom the judgment was entered (the Personnel Administrator of the Commonwealth and members of the Massachusetts Civil Service Commission) were opposed to an appeal and made their position known in writing. Governor Dukakis also went on record as opposing an appeal. Attorney General Bellotti did not agree, however, and as the chief legal officer of the Commonwealth, Bellotti felt that the decision was his to make. He lodged an appeal with the U.S. Supreme Court.

The first question before the court was whether or not Bellotti had the authority to appeal. The Supreme Court saw that as an unresolved question of Massachusetts law and sent the question to the Massachusetts Supreme Judicial Court for resolution.[17] The SJC came down on Bellotti's side.

> Where, in his judgment, an appeal would further the interests of the Commonwealth and the public he represents, the Attorney General may prosecute an appeal to the Supreme Court of the United States from a judgment of the District Court over the expressed objections of the State officers he represents.[18]

The appeal then went back before the U.S. Supreme Court, which reversed the decision and sent the case back to the District Court,[19] without writing an opinion, but with instructions that the court should reconsider the case in light of the Supreme Court's intervening decision in the case of *Washington v. Davis.*[20] In that case the Supreme Court upheld a District of Columbia pre-employment literacy test used by the police department, finding that the requirement was "reasonably and directly" related to the requirements of the police recruit training program, although not to actual job performance. The Court held that Fourteenth Amendment claims require proof of a discriminatory purpose, and that a statute is not unconstitutional solely because it has a disparate impact on a protected class of people.

The Supreme Court's remand for reconsideration in light of *Washington v. Davis* was an obvious indication that at least a significant portion of that court felt a different result was called for in the veterans' preference case. But on remand, Judges Tauro and Campbell decided the case the same way they had initially. Tauro again wrote the opinion of the court, stating that while disparate impact alone cannot establish a Fourteenth Amendment claim under *Davis,*

> [A]n invidious discriminatory purpose may often be inferred from the totality of relevant facts, including the fact, if it is true, that the law bears more heavily on one race than another...[21]
>
> ...The legislature was, at the least, chargeable with knowledge of the long-standing federal regulations limiting opportunities for women in the military, and the inevitable discriminatory consequences produced by their application to the challenged formula.[22]

The opinion fell on deaf ears. When Attorney General Bellotti again appealed to the Supreme Court, that Court again reversed, this time writing an opinion holding that the statute was constitutional. Justices Thurgood Marshall and William Brennan dissented.

Obviously, neither of the opinions authored by Tauro in the case went over well with most veterans. One found Tauro's number in the phone book, where it has always been, and registered his feelings directly.

Joe Tauro, William Brennan, June Tauro, and Mary Brennan

COURTESY OF HON. JOSEPH L. TAURO

Michael Ponsor: I was not the clerk on the case but I was there when the decision came out. A day or two later the judge told me that he had been at home the night before when the phone rang. He picked it up and a voice at the other end said scornfully: "Were you ever a veteran?"

"As a matter of fact I was," Tauro told him.

"What, with the Judge Advocate Corps?" said the voice.

"No, the artillery" said Tauro and then he called the man an epithet and slammed down the phone.

About 15 minutes later the phone rang again and Tauro answered. This time a somewhat chastened voice said: "That wasn't very nice, what you just said."

So the judge asked the man what he did for a living and it turned out he was a firefighter. The judge asked him: "Well, how would you feel if I called you up at home at night to complain about the way you had put out a fire? And besides, how would you feel if a daughter of yours tried to get a job in the Civil Service and was told she had no chance because she wasn't a veteran, even if she was well qualified?"

"I only have sons" said the man.

"Well, try to put yourself in the position of how you would feel if you had daughters," said the judge.

> Here was this guy who had called up to let the judge have it and Judge Tauro wound up engaging him and having a conversation on the phone. This is typical of the way he was: not intimidated, always himself in saying what he thought, and connecting with people.

First Amendment Rights

Judge Tauro's decision in the Boston State Hospital case had relied heavily on the First Amendment, protecting what Tauro saw as the individual's right to be free from mind-altering drugs. He would say later: "I really believe in this stuff—everybody's right to be left alone and everybody's right to speak his mind."

Over the years Tauro continued to defend the First Amendment in a variety of contexts, allowing broad latitude to anti-abortion protestors in one case, and in another case declaring unconstitutional a Massachusetts statute that barred media access to court records of cases in which the defendant was acquitted. Tauro ruled that such records could be sealed only on a case-by-case basis and only when the presiding judge made specific findings subject to review by an appellate court.

Perhaps Judge Tauro's most eloquent defense of the First Amendment came in a lawsuit over a book in the Chelsea High School library.[23] The book, *Male and Female Under 18,* was an anthology of writings by adolescents. The controversy concerned a poem in it entitled "The City to a Young Girl," written by Jody Caraviglia, a fifteen-year-old high school student in New York City. Caraviglia's poem describes city life to her as running a daily gauntlet of horny men verbally harassing her and begging for sexual favors. The poem's language is graphic, and when a complaining parent brought it to the attention of the Chelsea School Committee, a firestorm resulted. Led by its chairman, Andrew Quigley, publisher of *The Chelsea Record,* the school committee held a series of emergency meetings that resulted in banning the book and initiating an investigation of the process and the individuals responsible for its being in the library in the first place. Each step along the way was accompanied by editorials of outrage in the Chelsea paper.

The case came to trial in 1978, the same year that Judge Tauro heard the Boston State Hospital case. It was a bench trial that lasted six days before a packed courtroom.

> *Joe Tauro:* All these kids from Chelsea wanted to attend the trial, which I encouraged. They rented a couple of buses which brought them from Chelsea to the courtroom. There were too many kids to be able to sit down in chairs so I let them in and they sat Indian-style on the floor. The place was packed with kids from wall to wall. I remember the first day someone threw some toilet paper out of the bathroom window so I told everyone in court that I loved having them there, but don't ever do that again. They sat there and behaved. It was a study in participatory democracy.

Tauro's decision, handed down on July 5, 1978, held that the book could not be removed from the library, nor could the librarian be disciplined. He wrote:

> *City* is not a polite poem. Its language is tough, but not obscene. Whether or not scholarly, the poem is challenging and thought-provoking. It employs vivid street language, legitimately offensive to some, but certainly not to everyone. The author is writing about her perception of city life in rough but relevant language that gives credibility to the development of a sensitive theme. *City's* words may shock, but they communicate. As the Supreme Court has noted:
>
> > Words are often chosen as much for their emotive as their cognitive force. We cannot sanction the view that the constitution, while solicitous of the cognitive content of individual speech, has little or no regard for that emotive function which, practically speaking, may often be the more important element of the overall message sought to be communicated.[24]
>
> ...The most effective antidote to the poison of mindless orthodoxy is ready access to a broad sweep of ideas and philosophies. There is no danger in such exposure. The danger is in mind control. The Committee's ban of the anthology *Male & Female* is enjoined.[25]

Tauro's best-known First Amendment decision came a few years later, in a dispute over the mundane matter of a liquor license. The disappointed applicant was a Harvard Square restaurant, Grendel's Den. The restaurant's application for a liquor license had been denied by the Cambridge License Commission in accordance with a Massachusetts statute that required rejection if a church or school within 500 feet of the premises objected to its issuance. The Holy Cross Armenian Church had filed an objection, so the license was denied. Grendel's Den sued and the case was drawn by Judge Tauro.

The central legal issue in the *Grendel's Den* case was whether the state's delegation to churches of an absolute veto power over liquor licenses in specified circumstances amounted to a breach of the separation of church and state, in violation of the Establishment Clause of the First Amendment. In a prior challenge by another disappointed applicant, the Massachusetts SJC had ruled the same statute to be constitutional,[26] but Tauro was not bound by the SJC ruling in his application of federal constitutional law. Laurence Tribe, a renowned constitutional law expert from Harvard, argued the case for Grendel's Den. By the time the case was over, he would argue it four times: before Judge Tauro, who ruled for the plaintiff;[27] before a panel of the First Circuit Court of Appeals, which reversed;[28] again before the First Circuit, *en banc,* which disagreed with its own panel and affirmed Tauro;[29] and before the U.S. Supreme Court, which again affirmed.[30] The Supreme Court's opinion is a much-cited precedent in cases raising Establishment Clause issues. The Court stated:

Laurence Tribe

COURTESY OF LAURENCE H. TRIBE

> [T]he concept of a "wall" of separation [between church and state] is a useful signpost. Here that "wall" is substantially breached by vesting discretionary governmental powers in religious bodies.[31]

That was the same conclusion Judge Tauro had reached two years earlier. Tribe later commented that of all the judges he had appeared before in the *Grendel's Den* case, it was Tauro who best got to the heart of it.

> *Laurence Tribe:* He was right on target and saw exactly what was wrong with the law and why it differed from a liquor-free zone around a church, which had been upheld by the state's highest court. This was not a matter of the right to drink in Harvard Square, which would have been even more inhibited under a liquor-free zone, it was about the right not to live under the thumb of religious authority. Judge Tauro understood it perfectly, and rendered a very powerful opinion. The argument in front of him was fascinating. He asked just the right questions, probing the weaknesses of both sides. I felt afterward that I had been before someone who really understood what was at stake.

One of Professor Tribe's Harvard colleagues, Alan Dershowitz, is another admirer of Tauro. Dershowitz consulted with Tauro on a First Amendment case in the 1970s, when Tauro was still in private practice.

> *Alan Dershowitz:* It was the *I Am Curious Yellow* case, which ultimately went all the way to the Supreme Court. It was about a Swedish movie, which today would probably get a "GP" rating. It was an anti-war movie with a little nudity in it. The good folks of Massachusetts decided to put somebody in jail for showing it. The Symphony Cinema movie theater, right across from Symphony Hall, mostly showed boring Czechoslovakian movies, but it showed this one, and the power of the state came down heavy. I was retained to do the case, and I couldn't figure out what was going on, and who better to talk to than Joe Tauro. He was extremely helpful.
>
> He became a great innovative judge who set a standard that has been difficult to follow. What he did on behalf of the mentally ill in many ways shook up the state as much as any political figure has done, yet he did it in the context of cases and controversies and within the rules of judicial restraint. He came to the bench with such incredible knowledge of every aspect of Massachusetts—the political, the economic, and the legal—and he really took advantage of that.
>
> I did my best to try to get him appointed to the First Circuit later. It was in the late 1970s, toward the end of the Carter regime. They couldn't seem to get a Democrat nominated to fill a vacancy on the Court of Appeals, so I

> started a campaign to get Joe Tauro nominated. Who could be better? He was a moderate centrist, and the Republicans couldn't object because he was a Republican. I was pushing hard to get Joe appointed when one day he called to tell me to stop it. He said: "I'm pushing to get Steve Breyer appointed, so stop pushing me!"

George Thorogood

In 1991, Tauro drew another case that brought the press to his courtroom, but this time it was the arts and entertainment reporters. It was a copyright infringement action featuring rocker George Thorogood and his band, the Destroyers, a group with two platinum and a number of gold albums to their credit. The plaintiff, John Forward, claimed the copyright over demo tapes recorded by the band in 1975 when it was just starting out. Both sides sought injunctive relief to prevent the other from releasing the tapes.[32]

The trial began with a bang: Thorogood's "Move It On Over" rocked the packed courtroom. Thorogood's lawyer, Gordon Katz, argued that the tapes were of inferior quality and should not be released. He must have been a little worried when Tauro, who had admitted to being a big band fan, commented: "They're pretty good. You better stop playing the tapes or you're going to turn me into a big Thorogood fan just based on the tapes." In the end, Tauro found for Thorogood, ruling that Forward had not compensated the band or commissioned it to make the tapes, which therefore were not works made for hire for his benefit.

Ross Grimsley

Another case with its moment in the news involved another of Tauro's passions, baseball. It was not the national pastime at its finest. The events in question happened on September 16, 1975. The Boston Red Sox, on their way to the American League title and a World Series appearance against the Cincinnati Reds, were playing a game at Fenway Park against the second-place Baltimore Orioles. One Oriole who was having a rough year was pitcher Ross Grimsley. Grimsley, who had won eighteen games the previous year, had been relegated to the bullpen in the wake of several rough outings and a ballooning ERA. When he began to warm up, the fans in the bullpen area let him have it with some choice heckling. Grimsley seemed to be affected by it, and paused to look over at the hecklers two or three times. What happened next was a matter of dispute. On the last pitch of Grimsley's warm-up, either intentionally or by accident, he threw a ball, which went nowhere near the plate in the bullpen, but instead tore through the protective netting beside the bullpen and hit a fan, David Manning Jr., in the eye. Grimsley claimed the ball got away. Manning said it was a deliberate attempt to get back at hecklers who were sitting near him. Manning tried unsuccessfully to have Grimsley criminally prosecuted, but he also brought a civil suit against Grimsley and the Orioles. It was a jury case, presided over by Tauro, with ballplayers as witnesses and sports reporters providing press coverage. Tauro's clerk on the case was Donald Frederico. Frederico remembers a couple of notable moments from the case.

> *Don Frederico:* One was part of the cross-examination by Grimsley's lawyers. The witness was a guy named Elrod Hendricks, a catcher for the Orioles who must have been the bullpen catcher that day. Grimsley's lawyers were trying to undermine the plaintiff's lawyer's suggestion that Grimsley was likely particularly susceptible to the heckling because his ERA was so poor that year. It happened that in one game earlier that season the Orioles had been crushed, and their bullpen had been so depleted that in desperation they put Hendricks on the mound for an inning, and he managed to retire the side without giving up any runs. Consequently he had an ERA of 0.00. Grimsley's lawyer asked him: "So, does your 0.00 ERA mean you are a great pitcher?"
>
> I also remember getting a call during the trial from a law enforcement official from some town who said they had an outstanding warrant for Grimsley's arrest, which I think might have been on an unrelated matter, and they wanted to come to court to arrest him. I asked Judge Tauro about it and he told me: "Tell them to wait until after the jury returns its verdict," so that's what I did and that's exactly what happened.

The good news for Grimsley was that he prevailed on the civil case, at least in the trial court. Judge Tauro granted a defense motion for a directed verdict in their favor on the count of battery, and allowed the negligence count to go to the jury, which ruled for the defendants on that count as well. On appeal, however, a three-judge panel of the First Circuit unanimously reversed the directed verdict, holding that there was enough evidence of battery that it should have been allowed to go to the jury.[33] There were some familiar names on the opinion: Tauro's colleague Charles Wyzanski, sitting on the Appeals Court by designation on the case, who wrote the opinion, and Tauro's good friend Steve Breyer, who sat on the panel.

The Nantucket Sound Wind Farm Case

The environment was front and center in 2001 as a large group of litigants, lawyers, would-be interveners, interested bystanders, and the press showed up in Judge Tauro's courtroom for a couple of the early rounds in the fight over a proposal to build a wind farm in Nantucket Sound. The project was expected to generate enough electricity to meet seventy-five percent of demand on Cape Cod and the islands in an environmentally friendly way, but the prospect of 130 windmills towering hundreds of feet above the sound stirred a lot of local opposition.

While the proposed wind farm aroused passions on all sides, the issues before Judge Tauro in the two cases he heard in the matter were technical and dry. The first was the question of whether the project would require both a permit from the federal government and a license from the Commonwealth of Massachusetts. Tauro held that because the federal government had exclusive jurisdiction over the waters in question, only the federal permit was required.[34]

In the second case, project opponents challenged the federal permit issued by the Army Corps of Engineers. The case raised issues of statutory administration and administrative law. Judge Tauro denied the challenge. He agreed with the Army Corps of Engineers that it had jurisdiction to issue the permit, and he found that the requirements of the Environmental Protection Act had been satisfied in the process leading up to the permit. He also found that in any event, the Army Corps of Engineers had reasonably interpreted the statutes and regulations in question, and the court was therefore required to defer to its interpretations.[35] On appeal, the First Circuit Court of Appeals affirmed.[36]

Tauro noted in his opinions that the cases before him were only the first and second skirmishes in "what may prove to be a protracted struggle."[37] Subsequent skirmishes have taken place in a variety of forums ranging from local conservation commissions, the Cape Cod Commission, the Massachusetts Energy Facilities Siting Board, Massachusetts courts up to and including the Supreme Judicial Court, and the United States Department of the Interior. A new federal suit filed by project opponents in the Washington, D.C. federal court in June 2010, in the wake of Interior Secretary Ken Salazar's approval of the project, raised claims under the Endangered Species Act, the Migratory Bird Treaty Act, and the National Environmental Protection Act.

The Burma Law Litigation

Another case raised First Amendment issues in the context of political questions, but this time the context was the broad arena of foreign policy. *National Foreign Trade Council v. Baker*[38] involved a nonprofit trade association's challenge to a Massachusetts statute, the so-called "Burma Law," which prohibited Massachusetts and its agents from purchasing goods or services from anyone doing business with the Union of Myanmar, formerly known as Burma. The defense relied heavily on the state's first amendment interests in opposing human rights violations in Myanmar as a justification for the statute, but Judge Tauro held that "[s]tate interests, no matter how noble, do not trump the federal government's exclusive foreign affairs power" under the Constitution.[39] On appeal, a panel of the First Circuit Court of Appeals[40] and a unanimous U.S. Supreme Court[41] each came to the same conclusion.

Low-Profile Cases

It was Tauro's handling of some of the less-newsworthy cases that most stood out in the minds of some of his clerks:

> *Audrey Mark:* I'll never forget how Judge Tauro treated the civil litigants, especially the plaintiffs who were *pro se* and somehow disabled. I remember an elderly man who had been fired from his job. At a hearing on the defendant's motion to dismiss his case, the man was unable to articulate his position, and did not understand the law, but the Judge pointed out to defendant's counsel what a sympathetic witness the plaintiff

> would be at trial. The case ultimately settled, and the defendant paid an amount greater than a jury probably would have awarded. In my mind, the Judge made possible that equitable result by his kind words in the courtroom.
>
> I also remember a mentally ill woman who filed 10 or 15 complaints during my clerkship year. I think one of those complaints was a *habeas corpus* petition filed against the government that sought removal of certain dead bodies from a cemetery. Judge Tauro brought her in for a hearing, and although there was no possible relief he could have granted her under the law, he listened to her and spoke to her, and she seemed to feel better just having her day in court with him.

Settling Cases

Tauro's successful brokering of a settlement in *NAACP v. Boston Housing Authority,* and before that in the Belchertown and related cases, were a few examples among many of his role as a judge who often pushed settlement. In one complex environmental case, Tauro's reputation for settling cases caused Judge Woodlock to enlist Tauro's help in settling an intractable, multi-party litigation over the cleanup of a hazardous waste site, which had cost tens of millions of dollars.[42] In affirming the consent decrees in the case, the First Circuit applauded Woodlock and Tauro for their creative approach to settling the case and for their collaborative approach in working together in a case in which the trial judge did not feel he was in the best position to broker a settlement since he would have to decide the case if settlement efforts failed to resolve the case.[43]

Tauro has always encouraged parties in cases before him to settle, and he has not been shy about getting involved in the negotiations where the parties have gone along.

> *Joe Tauro:* When I was a young lawyer, we did a lot of our trials at Essex Superior Court in Salem. One of the judges who used to sit there a lot was George Jarvis Thompson. He had a great way of getting everyone in his chambers. The clerk would say, "The Judge thinks it's time for a cigarette. Anybody want to join him?" The lawyers would join him, and that would be the way to get people talking. The judge would say,

"Is there something I can do to help you resolve this?" That way nobody had to be the first one to bring up the subject of settlement. Lawyers are afraid that if they do that they will be perceived as weak. Some people say the trial judge shouldn't be involved in settlement, but it is certainly OK, in my opinion, to ask if there is anything you can do. If anyone says no, then there isn't anything, and you back off. But there always is. I never start a case without asking: Is there something I can do? What am I doing wrong? I try to make it light so that they can put down their armor and have a conversation.

You learn the importance of asking the right questions, and you learn where the soft underbelly of the case is. They go back and forth, but usually what they're arguing about is not the issue. Usually it's about money. That's where the cards come in. One of the first times I used them was in a big case that had Tommy Burns and Earle Cooley and a great cast of characters, all of whom hated each other for purposes of their case. My clerk at the time, Austin Jones, said to me that the parties were a million dollars apart, and no one was budging. I had them all come into my office, and I said to them that I wanted to find out how it was that such smart guys could be a million dollars apart. There's got to be something I am missing. I asked them each to put on a piece of paper the highest or lowest figure they would ever recommend. Forget about what the claims manager is going to say; what is the highest figure you, as trial counsel, would recommend. You are the one who has to go into the courtroom. Same thing for plaintiff's counsel. Make believe it's Sunday afternoon, and the trial starts tomorrow, and there's nothing you'd rather be doing than having a barbecue in the back yard and a couple of drinks. When they filled out the cards and gave them to me, they came back $75,000 apart. The case settled in about twenty minutes. I've done that many times since then—had the lawyers play my card game.

Of course everyone is concerned that their number will be the basis for further negotiations, so there is a temptation to high ball or low ball it, but I tell them to avoid that. Don't try to bullshit me. This may be your one chance to settle the case, and if the numbers are too far apart, then that is going to be the end of that. I've had that happen. The number has to be

> something I can work with. If one side is at $100,000 and the other is at $1,000, we are not going to settle that case. But more than likely those numbers are soft. Maybe the $100,000 is really $70,000, and maybe the $1,000 is really $55,000. Well, now I have something I can work with. Now we can have a conversation. Why are you so in love with your broken leg, or whatever it may be?

A former law clerk to Tauro, Frederick Brodie, shared his memories of this settlement practice in a letter to the judge:

> *Frederick Brodie:* I recall your practice of asking counsel to write on a 3x5 card their "no B.S." settlement number. You explained what you meant by that. The lawyers before you, by and large, seemed to know what to expect and appeared grateful for your efforts. Consequently, their no B.S. numbers appeared honest and unexaggerated. Indeed, in one conference, the two numbers turned out to be exactly the same. The case, of course, settled for that amount. After court, you told me that had never happened before. Some weeks later, you had a case in which the plaintiff's number was $10,000 lower than the defendant's number. You announced from the bench that the case would be settled for the defendant's number, and left the plaintiff's counsel silently to ponder the ways of fate.

Naturalization

Not everything a federal judge presides over is a case of controversy. Another role is to preside over ceremonies at which new citizens are naturalized. For Tauro, as for many federal judges, this is a duty but not a chore. As the grandson of an immigrant, he has an appreciation of what the occasion means to the participants and their families. One of those who was naturalized before Judge Tauro early in his tenure on the bench wrote about it in the *Christian Science Monitor,* in an article that came to the attention of the man who appointed Tauro:

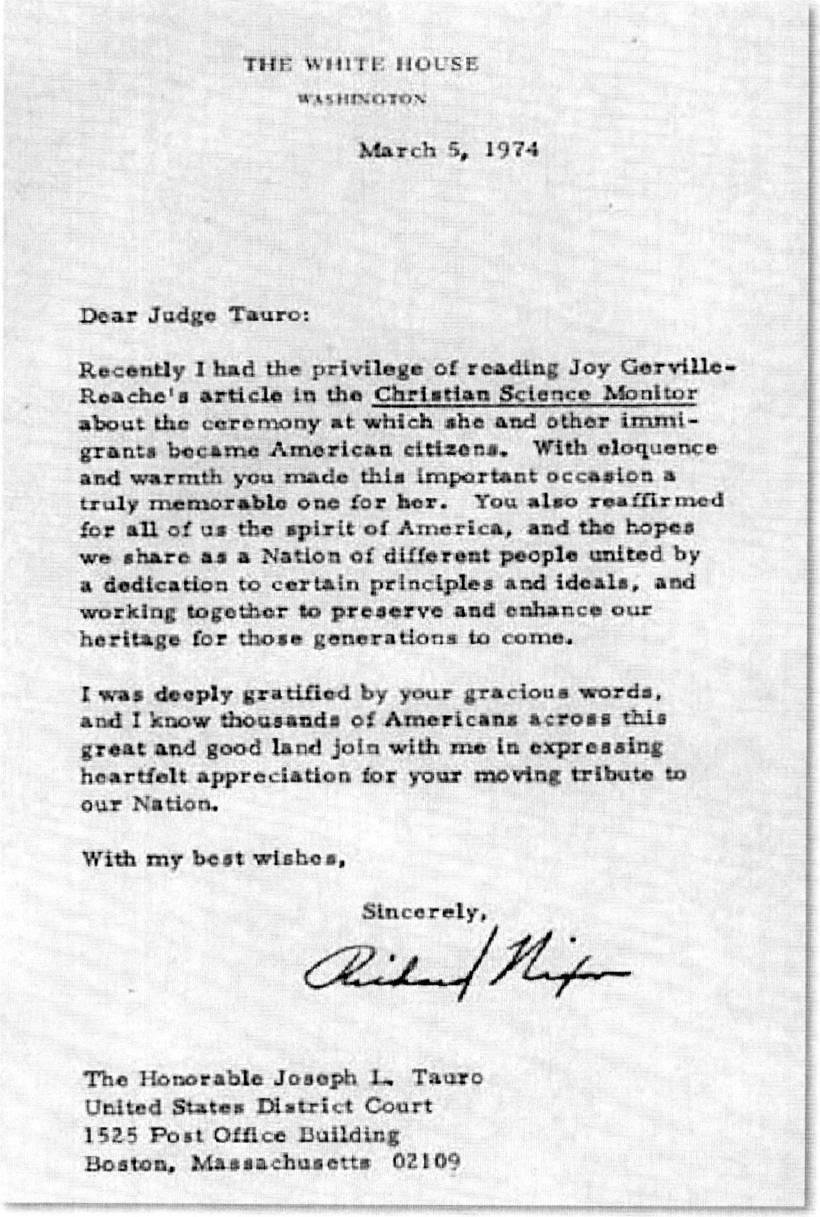

THE WHITE HOUSE

WASHINGTON

March 5, 1974

Dear Judge Tauro:

Recently I had the privilege of reading Joy Gerville-Reache's article in the Christian Science Monitor about the ceremony at which she and other immigrants became American citizens. With eloquence and warmth you made this important occasion a truly memorable one for her. You also reaffirmed for all of us the spirit of America, and the hopes we share as a Nation of different people united by a dedication to certain principles and ideals, and working together to preserve and enhance our heritage for those generations to come.

I was deeply gratified by your gracious words, and I know thousands of Americans across this great and good land join with me in expressing heartfelt appreciation for your moving tribute to our Nation.

With my best wishes,

Sincerely,

Richard Nixon

The Honorable Joseph L. Tauro
United States District Court
1525 Post Office Building
Boston, Massachusetts 02109

Letter to Judge Tauro from President Richard Nixon

COURTESY OF HON. JOSEPH L. TAURO

NOTES

1 *See Drinan v. Nixon,* 364 F. Supp. 854, 856 (D. Mass. 1973).

2 *Doe I v. Bush,* 240 F. Supp. 2d 95 (D. Mass. 2003).

3 *Id.* at 96.

4 421 F. Supp. 165 (D. Mass. 1976).

5 *Id.* at 188.

6 *Id.* at 192.

7 *See NAACP v. Boston Housing Auth.,* 723 F. Supp. 1554 (D. Mass. 1989).

8 *See* Elizabeth Neuffer, *NAACP, City Sign Pact to Pay Victims of Housing Bias,* BOS. GLOBE, Oct. 5, 1989, at 56.

9 996 F. Supp. 120 (D. Mass. 1998).

10 78 F.3d 932 (5th Cir. 1996), *rehearing en banc denied,* 84 F.3d 720, *cert. denied, Thurgood Marshall Legal Soc'y v. Hopwood,* 518 U.S. 1033 (1996).

11 *Wessmann,* 996 F. Supp. at 128.

12 *Wessmann v. Gittens,* 160 F.3d 790 (1st Cir. 1998).

13 *Id.* at 810 (Boudin, J., concurring).

14 451 F. Supp. 143 (D. Mass. 1978).

15 *Anthony v. Commonwealth,* 415 F. Supp. 485, 496 (D. Mass. 1970).

16 *Id.* at 499.

17 *See Massachusetts v. Feeney,* 429 U.S. 66 (1976).

18 *Feeney v. Commonwealth,* 373 Mass. 359, 366 (1977).

19 *See Massachusetts v. Feeney,* 434 U.S. 884 (1977).

20 426 U.S. 229 (1976).

21 *Feeney v. Commonwealth,* 451 F. Supp. 143 (D. Mass. 1978) (quoting *Washington v. Davis,* 426 U.S. at 242).

22 *Id.* at 148 (internal citations omitted).

23 *See Right to Read Defense Comm. v. Sch. Comm. of the City of Chelsea,* 454 F. Supp. 703 (D. Mass. 1976).

24 *Id.* at 714 (quoting *Cohen v. California,* 403 U.S. 15, 26 (1971)).

25 *Id.* at 715.

26 *See Arno v. Alcoholic Beverages Control Comm'n,* 377 Mass. 83 (1979).

27 *See Grendel's Den, Inc. v. Goodwin,* 495 F. Supp. 761 (D. Mass. 1980).

28 *See Grendel's Den, Inc. v. Goodwin,* 662 F.2d 88 (1st Cir. 1981).

[29] *See Grendel's Den, Inc. v. Goodwin,* 662 F.2d 102 (1st Cir. 1981) (en banc).

[30] *See Larkin v. Grendel's Den, Inc.,* 459 U.S. 116 (1982).

[31] *Id.* at 123.

[32] *See Forward v. Thorogood,* 758 F. Supp. 782 (D. Mass. 1991).

[33] *See Manning v. Grimsley,* No. 80-1145, 1981 U.S. App. LEXIS 19055 (1st Cir. Mar. 19, 1981).

[34] *See Ten Taxpayers Citizen Group v. Cape Wind Assocs.,* LLC, 278 F. Supp. 2d 98 (D. Mass. 2003).

[35] *See Alliance to Protect Nantucket Sound, Inc. v. U.S. Dep't of the Army* (Alliance I), 288 F. Supp. 2d 64 (D. Mass. 2003).

[36] *See Alliance to Protect Nantucket Sound, Inc. v. U.S. Dep't of the Army,* 398 F.3d 105 (1st Cir. 2005).

[37] *Alliance I,* 288 F. Supp. 2d at 66.

[38] 26 F. Supp. 2d 287 (D. Mass. 1998).

[39] *Id.* at 292.

[40] *See Nat'l Foreign Trade Council v. Natsios,* 181 F.3d 38 (1st Cir. 1999).

[41] *See Crosby v. Nat'l Foreign Trade Council,* 530 U.S. 363 (2000).

[42] *See United States v. Charles George Trucking Co., Inc.,* 682 F. Supp. 1260 (D. Mass. 1988).

[43] *See United States v. Charles George Trucking Co., Inc.,* 34 F.3d 1081 (1st Cir. 1994).

CHAPTER 11

The Criminal Docket

In the meantime, Judge Tauro's criminal docket was presenting its own challenges. One of his early cases went up to the U.S. Supreme Court and became a widely cited Fourth Amendment case.[1] A man and a woman had traveled by train from San Diego to Boston with two suitcases and a 200-pound footlocker. Federal agents in San Diego alerted their counterparts in Boston that they suspected the footlocker contained marijuana, based on the fact that it was leaking talcum powder, a substance sometimes used to mask the odor of marijuana. Also, the man traveling with the footlocker, Gregory Machado, fit a profile used by Amtrak to spot drug traffickers. When the couple arrived in Boston, a trained dog alerted agents to the presence of marijuana in the footlocker. In the meantime, a man named Joseph Chadwick arrived at South Station to pick up Machado and his female companion. Chadwick helped Machado lift the footlocker into the trunk of Machado's car. At that point, federal agents interceded, arrested all three people, and seized the car. An hour or two later, the agents searched the footlocker and the suitcases, without a warrant, and found marijuana in them all.

Chadwick challenged his arrest without a warrant. The issue before Judge Tauro was whether the agents had probable cause to arrest Chadwick. Tauro found that they did not, stating that it was at least as likely that Chadwick was innocently responding to the call of friends to pick him up at the train station as that he was an accomplice in a drug smuggling scheme. On appeal, the decision was affirmed; first by the First Circuit Court of Appeals,[2] and then by the U.S. Supreme Court in a 7-2 decision with Justices Blackmun and Rehnquist dissenting.[3]

As this and other Fourth Amendment rulings suggest, despite being an appointee of a President with a law-and-order reputation, and having himself served as U.S. Attorney, Judge Tauro was generally more popular with the defense bar than the prosecutors.

> *Joe Tauro:* I think if you ask the defense bar, they almost uniformly love me, but what I always say about the U.S. attorneys is that they may not like me so much while they're there, but when they leave and go into private practice, they'll be praying that they draw me.
>
> I've always made the government hold to the same standards as everybody else. To do the contrary is characteristic of some very pro-government judges. I am not that kind of person. I make the U.S. attorneys toe the mark. They have to do what everybody else does. They have to obey the rules. If they don't turn over papers critical to a trial then I'll interrupt the trial and recess it for two weeks, and first the defense will get the materials and then they can take depositions of the government witnesses so they are not prejudiced. I'm not the only one who does things like this—Judge Wolf, for example, is very strong on this. The U.S. attorneys know that I am not going to let them get away with anything, but I think they also know they are going to get a fair trial. I don't put my finger on the scales.

United States v. Pollock[4] was an early example of Judge Tauro's willingness to hold the government accountable for its failure to meet its pre-trial obligations. Pollock was charged with selling cocaine. He admitted the cocaine sale but said he was cooperating with the government in an effort to avoid or reduce the consequences from an earlier drug bust. He claimed that the cocaine sale at issue in the case before Tauro was done with the government's advance knowledge and approval in an attempt to set up a bigger transaction to follow, which would then be the subject of a government bust. The government acknowledged an agreement with Pollock for his cooperation, but claimed he had breached the agreement, and stated that they had neither authorized the cocaine sale in question nor offered to come to his aid if he was caught in such a sale.

The question before Judge Tauro on Pollock's motion to dismiss the indictment was: What were the terms of the government's arrangement with Pollock? Tauro initially denied Pollock's motion, believing the questions it raised should be decided by the jury, but a week before trial, Pollock's counsel brought to Tauro's attention a typewritten report that the government had just produced, purporting to set out the substance of the discussions nine months earlier between the government agents and Pollock. The report was dated two days after the discussions at which the cooperating arrangement was agreed.

Tauro's suspicions were aroused by the late appearance of the government's report, which was within a category of documents that defense counsel had requested much earlier and to which the defendant was undisputedly entitled. Additionally, the report tracked precisely the government's case, and specifically rebutted allegations made by Pollock, of which the government was unaware on the date of the report. Tauro postponed the trial and ordered an investigation of the circumstances of the preparation of the report, which led to the government's eventually admitting that: (1) the report had been prepared nine months after the fact and then backdated, and (2) at the time the report was prepared, a government agent destroyed his handwritten notes of the conversation with the defendant. Those notes were never provided to Pollock's counsel, even though they should have been. Tauro decided to dismiss the indictment against Pollock. He found that there was good reason to believe that the destroyed notes may have contained information exculpatory to Pollock on the central issue raised by his defense and that there was no way to afford Pollock a fair trial in their absence.[5]

Pollock was represented by Harvey Silverglate, who has gone on to a high-profile career as a criminal defense and civil liberties attorney. From Silverglate's point of view, the case turned out better than he ever expected.

> *Harvey Silverglate:* I thought the evidence was convincing that the government's original interview notes had been destroyed and the typewritten reports concocted more recently than their dates indicated, but I wasn't sure that the judge would find the facts honestly in a case in which the beneficiary of such fact-finding would be a defendant with a history of drug dealing. I was wrong. Judge Tauro called the facts precisely as he saw them. He wrote a powerful opinion dismissing the indictment, which was so persuasive that the government, which initially filed a notice of appeal, withdrew that appeal rather than risk a precedent in the First Circuit, not to mention a further admonition of the government's conduct in the case. My client, a then-young man with whom I

> maintained communications for many years thereafter, was so startled and impressed that a judge was willing to disbelieve federal drug agents and decide the case in an intellectually honest manner on the basis of the evidence, that he actually "went straight" and pursued an honest and productive career.

Lui Kin-Hong was another client of Silverglate and his firm, who drew Judge Tauro in his case—a *habeas corpus* petition, but not the usual challenge to a state court conviction. Lui was the former export director at the British American Tobacco Corporation in Hong Kong, which held exclusive rights to distribute cigarettes in certain Asian countries. Arrest warrants had been issued for him in Hong Kong, accusing him of soliciting and accepting bribes of over three million American dollars by a company seeking a monopoly over the export of certain brands of cigarettes. Lui and his family left Asia and became citizens of Canada. During a visit to Boston to see a friend, Lui was arrested in Boston, where he was held without bail pending extradition to Hong Kong pursuant to the request by the United Kingdom.

Extradition would have been a routine matter were it not for the fact that the United Kingdom's lease on Hong Kong was about to run out. There was no way that the United Kingdom would have time to try Lui and sentence him before the handover; rather, his fate would be up to the Chinese. China did not have a mutual extradition treaty, and, unlike the British, also did not have a criminal justice system that was familiar to and long-respected by the United States.

Lui argued that his extradition would be at odds with the extradition statute, which in his view, contemplated extradition only to a signatory to the extradition treaty, and only when that signatory would then be in a position to try and punish him. Judge Tauro agreed, writing a lengthy opinion which allowed the petition for *habeas corpus.*[6] On appeal, however, the First Circuit reversed, holding that the plain language of the statute compelled the Court to certify to the secretary of state that Lui could be extradited if the Secretary, at her discretion, chose to do so.[7] Lui sought further review in the U.S. Supreme Court, which denied his petition for certiorari, with Justices Breyer and Stevens dissenting.[8]

Tauro did not make a practice of dismissing criminal cases, but the *Pollock* case was not the only time he did it. In August 1982, in what was then the largest tax fraud case ever prosecuted in Massachusetts, after fifty-three days of trial

Judge Tauro ruled that there was insufficient evidence to send the case to the jury. The cases against all nine defendants were ordered dismissed, much to the prosecution's chagrin.

> *Joe Tauro:* The case went on all summer long. After the evidence closed, the lawyers argued the defense motion for a directed verdict. I went through the evidence and found that there was no evidence to support the government's theory, so I told the lawyers I was going to allow the motion. The lead government lawyer was a tax lawyer from Washington, and I remember him saying to me that the government had spent a million and a half dollars on the case, or whatever the number was. I told him it didn't matter to me if the government had spent five million. If you don't get to the jury, you don't get to the jury. You should have had evidence that got you to the jury.
>
> The government wanted to appeal my decision immediately. I told them I didn't think they could do that, but that I was prepared to hold the jury while we sent up to the U.S. Court of Appeals those parts of the record where the government claimed to have introduced the evidence that they said got them to the jury. That would give the Court of Appeals a chance to see if they thought I'd made a mistake or was being precipitous. Judge Bownes was on the U.S. Court of Appeals at that time, and the case went to him. I remember he kept the case almost the whole day while the jury was there, so I am assuming that he did some work on it, and then he sent it back and told me to dismiss the jury. And that was it. I had no axe to grind, and I wanted to make sure I wasn't making a horrible mistake. If the U.S. Court of Appeals even had jurisdiction to hear it at that point, I was happy to have them hear it.

Another case that Tauro technically did not dismiss, but which he might as well have, was a lower-profile case prosecuted by his future colleague, Rick Stearns.

> *Rick Stearns:* It was part of a Department of Justice initiative to crack down on cheating on Social Security benefits. The Department realized that there were thousands and thousands

Richard Stearns

COURTESY OF THE U.S. DISTRICT COURT FOR THE DISTRICT OF MASSACHUSETTS

of people collecting benefits who were dead. For some reason, the Social Security Administration had never matched the Social Security rolls against the death notices that the state maintains.

I had a case in which the defendant was an elderly and very sympathetic grandmother who herself was probably eligible for Social Security. It was one of these cases where you went for a settlement involving probation and restitution, not jail time. But I think Judge Tauro just felt it was too much power being brought to bear on this grandmother defendant. We were in court for what was going to be her guilty plea when Judge Tauro got up and left the bench and never came back! We were all ready to dispose of the case, but he did it for us. We wound up disposing of the case through an informal agreement with the woman, without a guilty plea.

One of the young assistant U.S. attorneys to try cases in front of Judge Tauro was Douglas Woodlock. Woodlock was well aware of Tauro's reputation within the office but he was nevertheless willing to take his chances before him.

Doug Woodlock: He had a very narrow target. Different judges have different views—it's a matter of strike zone, and his is very narrow. He was known to be particularly skeptical about circumstantial evidence and about conspiracy law. He also was fully prepared to direct verdicts or otherwise to narrow the case substantially. Still, he was incredibly principled, and I liked to try in front of him.

Douglas Woodlock

COURTESY OF THE U.S. DISTRICT COURT FOR THE DISTRICT OF MASSACHUSETTS

I did one case where the defense counsel was Judd Carhart, who had come from the U.S. Attorney's Office. Carhart brought a motion to suppress which Judge Tauro denied. Then Carhart said, "Let's go forward without a jury." He was throwing down the gauntlet to me. I said OK. I can't imagine an assistant U.S. attorney doing that now because they are afraid of doing anything without authority from the top, but

> [U.S. Attorney Edward] Harrington was not like that and we had much more leeway than they do now. I was thinking that it would take a long time to get a jury seated, that Tauro was ready to try the case, and maybe it was a little macho on my part to try a criminal case jury-waived in front of him.
>
> As it turned out the case only lasted a few hours and Tauro wound up finding for the defendant, but he did deny the motion for a directed judgment of acquittal and at least tried the case to a conclusion. So I went back to the office and I remember Harrington saying: what the hell did you do that for? What do you want to do, lose cases?

Robert Mueller, U.S. Attorney for Massachusetts and later FBI Director, offered his perspective on appearing before Tauro. Mueller was speaking at the portrait presentation for Judge Stearns in May 2006, hosted by Judge Tauro:

Robert Mueller

SOURCE: FEDERAL BUREAU OF INVESTIGATION WEB SITE

> *Bob Mueller:* It has been some time since I have actually been in a courtroom, but I do have memories of being in a courtroom, particularly your courtroom. If memory does serve me, appearing before you was only marginally better then being in front of a Congressional committee.

The Post Traumatic Stress Disorder Defense

The national press was back in Judge Tauro's courtroom in the fall of 1980 to watch as one of Boston's leading criminal defense attorneys, Joe Oteri, sought to be the first lawyer in the country to win an acquittal through a defense of post-traumatic stress disorder (PTSD). Oteri's client, Michael Tindall, faced drug smuggling charges. Tindall was a former Army helicopter pilot in the Vietnam War who had compiled an illustrious military record featuring two Distinguished Flying Crosses, two Bronze Stars, and a total of thirty-two air medals. Combat-induced trauma is, of course, a phenomenon as old as war, but there was little or no history of it being used successfully as a defense to criminal charges. The term

Joe Oteri

COURTESY OF JOE OTERI

"post traumatic stress disorder" did not come into use until 1980, the year Tindall went to trial.

Calling the PTSD defense "interesting and novel," Judge Tauro permitted Oteri to argue it to the jury.[9] Tauro also allowed Oteri considerable latitude in his efforts to establish it. At one point, over the prosecution's objection, Oteri was permitted to show the jury footage from the movies *The Deer Hunter* and *Apocalypse Now* in order to give them an appreciation for the horrors of the Vietnam War. Oteri argued that Tindall's experience in the war had turned him into an "action junkie" who was unable to resist opportunities to enjoy thrills, and that Tindall's drug-smuggling activities were the direct result of that. In the end, the jury agreed. Tindall was acquitted. Oteri said later that "there wasn't another judge in America who would have allowed me to defend the case that way."

The Tindall case set a precedent, but it hardly opened a floodgate. Despite dozens of subsequent cases in which defense attorneys argued PTSD defenses, in only two other cases over the next twenty-five years did the jury accept it.

The Kelly Mistrial and Motion to Recuse

Perhaps the time when Tauro most upset the prosecution, however, was not a dismissal but a declaration of mistrial. It was 1981, the year after the Tindall trial. The defendant, James Kelly, former chairman of the Massachusetts Senate Ways and Means Committee, was accused of extorting $34,000 from an architect in connection with a contract with the state. Kelly was a big name, and the case was a centerpiece in the government's effort to crack down on political corruption and bribery. At side bar during the trial, Judge Tauro made no secret of his skepticism of the government's case against Kelly, saying at one point that if he, rather than the jury, were the fact finder, he would acquit Kelly without hesitation. At another point, he said he wouldn't give 50¢ for $50 of testimony from Frank Masiello, a cooperating witness who was at the heart of the government's case.

Despite his dim view of the government's case against Kelly, Tauro did elect to let the case go to the jury after a twenty-five-day trial. His jury charge, however, did not sit well with the government. Tauro told the jury that the testimony of five immunized witnesses should be taken with more than a grain of salt, maybe even a box of salt. Also, if the jurors did not unanimously believe the testimony of Frank Masiello, they should go no further in their deliberations.

Jury deliberations did not go smoothly, resulting in a series of notes from the jury to the judge reporting deadlock. One of these notes told the court what was going on in the jury room.

> *Joe Tauro:* I had a note from the jury about deadlock, and I asked the lawyers for their position about what I should do about it. At that point I thought the government was losing the case, and I think the prosecutor, [Lloyd] Macdonald, must have thought so too because he wanted to start over. Then I turned over the note and on the other side there was an explanation that the jury was 11-1 to convict, with the lone holdout being a woman who said she was never going to change her mind. I told the lawyers what the note said and at that point Macdonald, of course, changed his tack and began to argue strenuously that I should send the jury back out to continue deliberating while the defense attorney, George MacLaughlin, pushed for a mistrial.
>
> I'm not sure if it was at this point or a later point where the jury had again reported a deadlock, but I remember being in the robing room, getting ready to go out on the bench, and telling my law clerk, Howard Pearl, that I thought the time had come to call a mistrial. He told me: "Why don't you give it one more shot?" He persuaded me to do that.

In the end, the jury was sent back several times, to no avail. After thirteen hours of deliberations, Judge Tauro declared a mistrial. Macdonald was not happy at what he felt was a premature dismissal of the jury, but his boss, U.S. Attorney Edward Harrington, was furious. Harrington's unflattering epithets about Judge Tauro were overheard by a reporter in the courthouse corridor and found their way into the newspaper. Tauro responded, saying that he had learned as a boy that you shouldn't blame the umpire when you strike out.

> *Joe Tauro:* Ted and I have been colleagues on the bench for many years now, and he's a good friend, but that was a rough time between us.

Edward Harrington

COURTESY OF THE U.S. DISTRICT COURT FOR THE DISTRICT OF MASSACHUSETTS

The press had followed the Kelly trial closely and as it came to a head: a couple of columns appeared in the newspapers suggesting that Judge Tauro appeared to be biased in favor of the defendant because of events fifteen years earlier. In the 1960s Senator Kelly, a Democrat, had headed a committee that investigated charges of kickbacks under the administration of Governor Volpe. Tauro had been Volpe's chief counsel at the time of the committee investigation. The theory of the newspaper columns was that Tauro had served as Volpe's liaison to the committee, and that Kelly had caused the committee to issue a favorable report, creating a debt that Tauro was repaying as judge fifteen years later.

In the wake of the mistrial and the newspaper columns, the government brought a motion seeking to have Judge Tauro recuse himself from sitting on the new trial.

Judge Harrington laughs about it now.

> *Ted Harrington:* We wanted to get rid of him. Who wouldn't? We wanted to win the case.

Assistant U.S. Attorney Woodlock was assigned to bring the motion. Tauro denied it in a long opinion.

> As has been detailed by me in the accompanying memorandum, an investigation conducted by the F.B.I. has established that in fact no relationship ever existed between the defendant and me, let alone one that would meet the standards for a disqualification motion. It is now clear that the U.S. attorney's motion to disqualify me was based on innuendo and rumor and that it was not 'grounded on facts' or on 'probative evidence.'[10]

In the same order denying the motion, Tauro referred the matter to the First Circuit Court of Appeals for review. In due course the First Circuit denied the appeal.

> *Joe Tauro:* Gael Mahoney was my lawyer on that, which the government paid for, since usually it would be the U.S. Attorney's Office that represented a federal judge, but they were on the other side of this. He ferreted out every piece of information, and what he showed was that Kelly had not favored Volpe in the probe fifteen years earlier, but in fact it was just the reverse. Kelly was the one in committee meetings who had been hardest on Volpe, but you didn't find that in the newspapers.
>
> What I told everybody was that the whole idea that I was somehow in cahoots with Kelly just made no sense. Relations with the legislature weren't my job— that was up to others. As Volpe's chief legal counsel I dealt with policy issues, and I really only dealt with the governor and his senior advisors.

Tauro stayed proceedings in the Kelly matter during the period when the First Circuit was deciding the appeal of the motion to vacate. When the appeal was denied, the first order of business was the defendant's pending motion to dismiss the case based on alleged prosecutorial misconduct at the trial. The claim was that the prosecutor, Lloyd Macdonald, had put on a witness, William Masiello, to testify in ways that Macdonald knew to be false. Tauro agreed with the defense claim, finding that Macdonald had acted unethically, but he did not agree with the proposed remedy.

At this point another future colleague of Tauro's got involved in the proceedings.

> *Mark Wolf:* I had come to the U.S. Attorney's Office in 1981 as chief of the Public Corruption Unit. This was one of my early appearances as a federal prosecutor, and I was representing the government at what was a perilous time for a high-stakes case. The argument happened the day my son graduated from nursery school. I went to the graduation in the morning, and then I had to excuse myself from the picnic afterwards. I remember telling Jonathan that I had to leave to go argue a

> case in court, and Jonathan saying to me: "But Daddy, it's not nice to argue."

> *Joe Tauro:* Mark Wolf did not accept that there had been any misconduct, but he also argued that if the court were to find otherwise, the appropriate remedy would not be to dismiss the case, but rather to refer the matter to the disciplinary arm of the bar. That made sense to me and that's what I did. I sent the matter to the Board of Bar Overseers.

Robert Meserve represented Macdonald before the Board of Bar Overseers (BBO), which issued a decision finding that Macdonald had not committed any intentional wrongdoing.

> *Mark Wolf:* Judge Tauro had published his decision, referring Macdonald's case to the BBO, in the reported decisions published by West. When the BBO issued its decision, I filed something before Judge Tauro asking that he have the BBO decision reported next to his original decision so that the record would be complete, which he did.

Thus vindicated, Macdonald, then running for Suffolk County District Attorney against Newman Flanagan, was quoted in the press as saying that Tauro's referral of the case to the BBO had been "a spiteful act of a small federal judge seeking to get revenge." Macdonald's outburst was the culmination of a series of clashes in the high-stakes Kelly trial.

The breach between Tauro and Macdonald did not prove permanent, however.

> *Joe Tauro:* Several years later Lloyd Macdonald was said to be a serious candidate for U.S. Attorney. Some enterprising reporter for the *Globe* called me and asked me if I had any comment about the reports of his candidacy. I said that as far as I was concerned he had outstanding qualifications. He was a terrific trial lawyer and he would be a great U.S. Attorney. The reporter asked me about my experience with him on the Kelly case, and I said that was one case a long time ago. I said I

thought he was a very capable guy who would do a wonderful job.

The next day there was a story in the paper reporting my comments. After that, Lloyd Macdonald wrote me the nicest letter. He said that for all these years he had been ashamed of the way he had talked about me after the trial, that it was very unprofessional of him and unfair. He said he was very grateful for my kind comments.

I wrote Lloyd a note to thank him for his, and I invited him to lunch. We had a nice, cordial lunch in my chambers. There were no hard feelings for either of us.

Ilario Zannino, Mobster With a Bad Heart

Overlapping with the Kelly saga was another even longer-running affair: the efforts of law enforcement to bring to justice Ilario "Larry Baione" Zannino, the number two guy in the Boston branch of the organized crime family run by Raymond Patriarca. Zannino reported to the top Boston mobster, Gennaro Angiulo. Zannino was reported to have a wallet that looked like the inside of a bank vault and a gambling and loan-sharking business more successful than the leading car companies.

When federal agents caught up with Zannino in the late 1970s, his primary defense to the criminal charges he faced was heart problems. He had been hospitalized in 1977 for congestive heart failure, and over the following years there was a series of further hospitalizations for heart problems. At the time there were pending charges against him in both state and federal courts.

Tauro had the federal case, and the threshold issue before him was whether Zannino was healthy enough to stand trial. Zannino and the government both put on expert testimony to address that issue.

Joe Tauro: It turned out by coincidence that Zannino's doctor, Meyer Halperin, was my doctor. Meyer Halperin was a very good doctor in the Lynn area. The only reason he had Zannino as a patient was that it was Meyer's turn in the emergency room one day when Zannino was taken in there as an emergency patient, so he wound up as Zannino's doctor and was called upon in connection with the case. I explained

> to everybody that Halperin was my doctor and asked them if they wanted me to recuse myself, but nobody did, so I stayed in. Halperin was an honest guy and he was not a player. He gave a solid opinion and he turned out to be right.

Actually it did not turn into a battle of the experts because the government's expert, the chief of emergency medicine at Massachusetts General Hospital, agreed with Dr. Halperin that there was a substantial likelihood that the stresses of the trial would trigger another heart attack for Zannino. Accordingly, Tauro elected to postpone the trial indefinitely, telling the government to come back if and when there was a change in Zannino's medical situation.

In August 1980, Zannino was arrested again on bookmaking charges, causing U.S. Attorney Edward Harrington to comment that bookmaking must be easy because it seemed to be less strenuous than appearing in court.[11] The following May there was more of the same, when Zannino was arrested with fourteen others at Angiulo's North End office as they were getting ready to sit down to a late night dinner of chicken cacciatore and linguini. Harrington was quoted as saying that he was "shocked and dismayed by this arrogant affront to the judicial process."

> *Ted Harrington:* I was frustrated. I wanted to get this guy because next to Gerry Angiulo he was the most powerful organized crime figure in the greater Boston area. He was the muscle in the Angiulo group and a very tough individual.

A couple weeks later, as Marvin Hagler successfully defended his middleweight title at Boston Garden in a fifth-round TKO over former champ Vito Antuofermo, Zannino was there, along with the press. The cops asked him sarcastically: "Feelin' all right, Larry?"

"Ya, and I'm going to outlive every one of you bastards," said Zannino.

Zannino was not making Tauro look good, but the judge was unmoved, commenting in court: "If he wants to die at ringside, that may be something that will happen."

In September 1993, Zannino was indicted again, as part of a mob-busting series of indictments that included Gennaro Angiulo and two of Angiulo's brothers. On the day the indictment was returned, Zannino was hospitalized, complaining of chest pain. This time Zannino drew a different federal judge, David Nelson. The government brought in a new expert to address the issue of Zannino's health, a New York doctor who testified that there was no established link between stress and heart attack. Finding that the risk of cardiac arrest was remote, and that Zannino's angina and congestive heart failure were treatable with proper medication and diet, Nelson, relying on a report and recommendation from Magistrate Judge Joyce Alexander, allowed the case to go forward.[12]

On the day the trial started, Judge Nelson called Judge Tauro. A few minutes later, he called him a second time.

> *Joe Tauro:* The day they were going to trial, I was in my backyard sitting by the pool. Why I took the day off I don't remember. I got a call from Dave Nelson. He wanted me to know that he was going forward with the trial, and he meant no disrespect to me because I had said Zannino was too sick to stand trial. I told him: "David, I think you are making a mistake, but you are really a great guy to call me, and I am not affected in any way. That was very nice of you to call." And that was it. Then about twenty minutes later he called me again and said: "Joe, you're a genius!" He said that Zannino had suffered another heart attack, and they had him in the corridor outside of the courtroom.

Zannino didn't even make it through the opening statements before he was hospitalized. When he appeared to recover soon thereafter, the trial continued, but six days later Zannino suffered a second myocardial infarction, forcing the government to sever his case as they proceeded with the trial against the Angiulos.

In the end, the government did finally manage to bring Zannino to justice, three years later. Following the advice of a panel of three renowned cardiologists, he was tried on reduced charges, with strict conditions: abbreviated trial days, periodic mid-trial examinations, continuous monitoring by electrocardiogram while in the courtroom, instant availability of emergency medications and supplies, and the presence of medical personnel at trial. The trial was punctuated by a week-long hiatus for medical tests, but it was eventually completed, and the resulting guilty verdicts were enough to put Zannino in prison for the last ten years of his life.

John Connolly, FBI Agent

Judge Tauro's handling of another high-profile organized crime related case went over better with the prosecution. The defendant, John "Zip" Connolly, was a former FBI agent who for years had used a kingpin of the Boston mob, James "Whitey" Bulger, as a confidential informant. Bulger and Connolly grew up as friends in the same Boston housing development. Bulger fed Connolly information which led to investigations and arrests of rival mobsters. But according to the indictment, Bulger also paid Connolly bribes, and Connolly in turn passed on to Bulger information about other informants who were a threat to Bulger. At least a couple of those informants ended up dead as a result. Connolly was also charged with tipping off Bulger to his impending arrest, enabling Bulger to flee and escape capture despite years on the FBI's "Most Wanted" list until he was finally caught in 2011.

John Connolly

PRINTED WITH PERMISSION OF ASSOCIATED PRESS

In the spring of 2002, Connolly went to trial before Judge Tauro on charges of racketeering and obstruction of justice. An early ruling by the judge, which allowed Connolly to sit in the gallery with his wife and children during opening statements, did not please the prosecution, but to the judge it was routine.

> *Joe Tauro:* In all cases I let the parties sit wherever they want. If they want to sit in the well where the lawyers sit, then they have to ask permission. It may be automatic, and maybe no one ever turns the request down but you have to ask. But other than that they can sit any place. Connolly said that he wanted to sit in the audience with his family, and my ruling was that he could sit wherever he wanted but wherever he starts, that's where he stays during the whole trial. So he sat there for the whole trial, except for the day he was going to be sentenced. Then I sent word to his lawyer that I wanted him at

> counsel table because I knew I was going to send him to jail. I didn't want to have somebody going into the spectators to haul him out.

However, on the major evidentiary issue—whether the evidence of the resulting murders could come in to help prove the nature of the relationship between Connolly and Bulger—Tauro ruled that it could.

> *Joe Tauro:* My inclination at the beginning was that it wouldn't come in. It's hearsay, too remote, prejudicial. Then I gave them an opportunity to argue it, and the prosecutor persuaded me that it should come in.

On May 28, 2002, Connolly was convicted. In the sentencing proceedings that followed, over 200 individuals submitted letters in support of Connolly, including Edward Harrington, who by then was a federal judge and Tauro's colleague. Harrington had served as U.S. Attorney during some of the period when Connolly was providing information from Bulger that led to some important convictions, and Harrington lauded Connolly for his efforts in connection with those prosecutions. Judge Tauro was unswayed by the letter campaign, however, and he sentenced Connolly to ten years in prison, the maximum allowable. Tauro cited in particular Connolly's efforts to subvert the judicial process by threatening and intimidating witnesses, saying that Connolly's actions "attacked the very heart of what we attempt to do every day in this building: administer justice fairly."

Tauro's sentence was not the last word in the case. Three years later, Connolly's lawyers filed an extensive motion for a new trial. The heart of the motion was an affidavit from a man who had spent time in prison with Francis "Cadillac Frank" Salemme, a former associate of Bulger. Salemme had testified at the Connolly trial that Connolly warned Salemme, Bulger, and another associate, Steven "The Rifleman" Flemmi, about the FBI's plans to arrest them. In prison later, Salemme allegedly told a cellmate that his testimony against Connolly was false and that he had "outslicked" prosecutors to help send Connolly to prison.

Tauro reviewed the motion for a new trial and denied it, writing the single word "denied" in the margin of the first page of the motion, as judges sometimes do.

> *Joe Tauro:* It was a mammoth motion, with what was like a telephone book full of objections. I read it all, but I didn't want to dignify it with a long discussion or let myself get drawn into minutiae. I had the right to just say "denied," which made it very clear that as far as I was concerned, there was no basis anywhere in the record for relief. Very often I do that—if I'm going to deny something, I just say "denied." It's very clear and it saves a lot of time. When we had judges' meetings with the bar, Bill Young used to quote me on this. He'd tell lawyers: "As Joe Tauro would say, what part of the word "denied" don't you understand?" I've got plenty to write about without writing about something I don't have to.

Connolly's attorney was furious at Tauro's denial of his motion without an opinion, telling the press that he was shocked. The outburst did not go over well with one of Tauro's colleagues on the court.

> *Joe Tauro:* When one of the defense attorneys knocked me in the press, Bill Young, who was then the chief judge—without me saying anything to him—reported the matter to the bar association. Lawyers are not supposed to openly criticize a judge in the newspapers, especially about a pending matter, but we let it go.

Sentencing

Connolly's sentence was an aberration from Judge Tauro's usual practice. Judge Tauro was typically not a fan of harsh sentences in criminal cases. In describing his philosophy on sentencing, he wrote:

> I see jail as a certain instrument for punishment but a doubtful vehicle for rehabilitation. The merit of jail as a means for realizing the third sentencing objective, deterrence, is less clear.... It is a matter of pure speculation to predict with any accuracy the deterrent effect of any sentence.[13]

Tauro commented that he had toured just about every type of federal prison in the county and had yet to see a "country club" type prison, as those who complained of soft sentences were want to invoke.[14] He found that prisons were mostly "just human warehouses."

> Joe Tauro: I have adopted what I call the "least drastic alternative" as my sentencing philosophy. If I think that five years will do the job as well as ten, I give the five-year sentence. If there is an improved attitude toward society, I'll give a suspended sentence.

Tauro has always felt strongly that the sentencing judge had an important role to play and needs the discretion to play it effectively.

> *Joe Tauro:* I don't think we do anything more important or significant as judges than to look somebody in the eye and decide whether he is going to go to jail. Even when you are facing someone who has a really despicable record, you want to make sure that you are being fair and objective with this person, and that you are not unduly punishing him for what he did. When I finally pass sentence I want to know the whole man or woman before me.... I take the file home and read it carefully three or four times. One factor I give heavy consideration is the presence or absence of a genuine sense of sorrow—contrition.

Sentencing is one part of the job that Tauro does not enjoy.

> *Michael Ponsor:* In general, the pressures of the job did not get to him. I remember him one time saying to me: "I am never overwhelmed by my work."
>
> The one exception was sentencing: he had no appetite for putting people in jail. He was just never one who enjoyed sinking his fangs into someone's neck. I remember one case where he sent a young guy to prison for what we would consider a fairly modest sentence, maybe two or three years. As we were riding up in the elevator to return to his chambers, he turned to me and said: "I hate this damn job!" Sentencing really weighed on him.

Not surprisingly, Tauro was not happy when the law was changed to establish rigid sentencing guidelines, which he viewed as usurping the district court's proper role in sentencing—although he does favor narrowing statutory sentencing ranges enough to eliminate radically disparate sentencing results for similar cases.

> *Joe Tauro:* I would have changed the way it was when I was first on the bench, so that instead of making a first offense punishable by 0–15 years maybe it would be 0–3. I never felt there was a particular discrepancy between the judges on sentencing. But I would never have made it formulaic, the way it was after the guidelines came in. It got to be just a question of math. I was embarrassed when that was the way it was because most of the arguments about sentencing were all about math—plus two for this, minus two for that. The poor defendant would be just sitting there wondering what's happening with his life. He doesn't understand plus two minus three.
>
> Now we're back to a situation where there is a lot more discretion in sentencing because of the decision Justice Breyer wrote. What the court said is that the guidelines are just that, guidelines. I welcome that. It makes it closer to the way it was when I went on the bench.

Tauro's humane view of criminal defendants was not born on the bench—he had shown it earlier as a prosecutor.

> *Joe Tauro:* When I was an assistant U.S. attorney, about twenty-seven years old, the Criminal Division was headed by Bill Cohen, who was a real old pro. In those days, the defendants didn't necessarily have counsel, and you talked to them directly. It was a very pro-cop environment. Cohen gave me a case that involved somebody who was head of a school committee someplace, who had been taking pornographic photos of himself and sending them to friends and getting them back. He got caught. He was married, he had kids, and he was very, very embarrassed. I took all of this information down and went to talk to Cohen about it. He asked me what I thought and I told him: I think we should let him off the hot

seat and not prosecute him. Cohen told me: good, you've shown that you have some judgment. Always remember with a guy like that, if he screws up, you'll see him again. There was no sense in destroying this guy's life over a few photographs that they were using to titillate each other. You don't have to be too tough. You have to be tough enough, but you don't have to overdo it. I always thought about that.

Tauro had a similar experience with Judge George Sweeney. Sweeney was the chief judge of the federal court when Tauro was an assistant U.S. attorney. He was an old-timer who had been appointed to the federal bench by Franklin Roosevelt.

Joe Tauro: I was handling the prosecution of some guy who I think had stolen a car. I felt bad for the guy because he was headed to prison for what could be a very long time. In those days defendants didn't always have counsel, and this guy was going to be on his own at the sentencing with me as the prosecutor. I asked to see Judge Sweeney, being young and not realizing that wasn't done. I went in to his office and told him that he was going to have this sentencing. I told him I thought the defendant was a terrific guy who had made a mistake. He looked at me through his cigar smoke and said: "Tauro, you're soft. Stay that way."

George Sweeney (left) at Joe Tauro's swearing in as U.S. Attorney for the District of Massachusetts

COURTESY OF HON. JOSEPH L. TAURO

Doug Woodlock: Sweeney was the judge who sentenced Ray Charles when drug charges were brought against him here. The U.S. Attorney was looking for a lot of time, and Sweeney put him in a

> drug treatment program and he was able to turn his life around.

Tauro's sentences frequently included a large component of public service work as an alternative to prison.

> A meaningful, closely supervised public service sentence can provide a daily reminder to the offender that he has in fact committed serious anti-social behavior. It gives the offender an opportunity to pour some water back into the public well—to redeem himself both in his own eyes and in the eyes of his fellow man.[15]

Predictably, Judge Tauro's approach to sentencing was much more popular with the defense bar than with the U.S. Attorney's Office. Edward Harrington was one U.S. Attorney who was a vocal critic of Tauro's leniency. As it turned out, Harrington would join Tauro on the federal bench in 1988—the same year Judge Tauro was given a Judicial Achievement Award by the National Association of Criminal Defense Attorneys. In accepting the award, Tauro told the defense attorneys: "Ours is a noble profession. Lawyers make a real difference for the people of this country. Don't ever forget that, and don't let anyone else forget it either.... Have the courage to be unpopular."

When alternate sentencing worked as Tauro hoped, the results were gratifying.

> *Joe Tauro:* I had a case involving two B.C. students who had sold a large amount of marijuana at their college. They had no prior records. After a lot of consideration I decided to sentence them to a three-year suspended sentence with sixty hours a month of public service, closely supervised by parole officers. This kind of sentence is common now, but was very rare back then.
>
> Several years later, I taught a class or a moot court at Suffolk University on Beacon Hill. One night when it was over, I was walking back, and it was very dark, and this big young guy came up to me on a quiet street and said: "You're Judge Tauro, aren't you?"

I didn't like the looks of the situation, but I said "Yes," trying to act like I was 6'3" instead of what I am.

He said: "I'm so and so. I don't know if you remember me. I was at B.C. and you sentenced me to probation and to serving my probation by working at the Fernald School. You saved my life. They let me finish law school, and I just passed the bar. I just want to tell you that I will never forget you."

I remember his case. It was the first time I had used a public service sentence. I talked with Bill Hogan, the Chief Probation Officer, who had been around forever, and I told him: "I hate to send this kid to jail. It's a serious offense, but it's his first offense. Is there any way I can salvage him, making him do something like public service?" Hogan asked me what I had in mind. I suggested having the kid work at the Fernald School for a year as a condition of his probation. I asked if that was legal. Hogan thought it was legal, and suggested that I should make the service conditional and have the kid agree to it as a condition of his probation so it wouldn't be construed as involuntary servitude. I was a little worried about that. I didn't want to have the kid be a wise guy and wiggle out. After that, there were many times that I gave sentences that involved public service and my colleagues started doing it too.

Another time I was driving down the street and a nice-looking kid with a woman beside him and a couple of kids in the back seat pulled up alongside me and called out: "Judge Tauro!" It was another kid I had sentenced. He had been sent to prison in Kentucky and at one point when he was back on some sort of leave he had lodged a complaint about the prison conditions in Kentucky. I tried to get him released, but the Court of Appeals reversed me on a technicality. But it was nice that this kid recognized me. He said: "My wife. My kids."

Richard Hart was another defendant who took advantage of the opportunity afforded by a Tauro sentence to turn his life around. Hart was one of eighteen people involved in a scheme to smuggle 15,000 pounds of marijuana into Cape Cod. Judge Tauro handed down one of the lightest sentences possible: a two-year suspended sentence, one year of supervised probation, and two years of special parole. Several years after completing his sentence Hart went on to become the extremely successful head of the Chatham Seafood Exchange.

Inevitably, not every recipient of an alternative sentence proved to be a poster boy for the success of the program. In July 1977, Abe Sarkis, a long-time bookie associated with organized crime and well known in Boston gambling circles, faced Tauro for sentencing. Sarkis admitted his offenses and promised he would never accept another bet. "At my age," he told Tauro, "I'm all through. I have grandchildren." Tauro gave Sarkis a suspended sentence and parole, on the condition that he perform community service at Fernald.

By all accounts Sarkis performed well there, but he was arrested again the following spring for illegally keeping an M-1. He insisted before Tauro that he was a changed man. Tauro again let him go on probation, to run concurrently with his probation in the gambling case. In the summer of 1980, just sixteen days after his probation expired, he was arrested again and charged with using gaming apparatus to register bets. Apparently retirement had not agreed with him.

Of course not every criminal case was high-profile. There was plenty of everyday stuff, and there were at least a couple of criminal cases that must have given Tauro a sense of how Wyzanski felt about some of the cases that came before him. Tauro's colleague, Nancy Gertner, recalls one, and a former law clerk, Roderick MacLeish Jr., recalls another.

> *Nancy Gertner:* In my twenty-three years as a lawyer, I only appeared before Judge Tauro once. I was representing a man who had taken a $70 welfare check out of his neighbor's mailbox. Tauro thought the prosecution was preposterous. He announced, sarcastically: "I promised myself when I became a judge that I would never criticize the U.S. Attorney if he brought a case involving a theft of say, over $69.99, so I won't." The point was made. My client was sentenced to a single day—the one spent waiting for his case to be called.

> *Roderick MacLeish:* Early in my clerkship, I remember sitting in court while Judge Tauro presided over a case involving the prosecution of a janitor who had allegedly stolen some $500 worth of towels from a veteran's hospital. After spending a week or so on this matter, the Judge decided it would be appropriate to have then U.S. Attorney (now Judge) Harrington down for a discussion to explain why it was in the

interests of the U.S. Attorney to continue with the prosecution.

NOTES

[1] *See United States v. Chadwick,* 393 F. Supp. 763 (D. Mass. 1975).

[2] *See United States v. Chadwick,* 532 F.2d 773 (1st Cir. 1976).

[3] *See United States v. Chadwick,* 433 U.S. 1 (1997).

[4] 417 F. Supp. 1332 (D. Mass. 1976).

[5] *See id.* at 1349.

[6] *See Lui Kin-Hong v. United States,* 926 F. Supp. 1180 (D. Mass. 1996).

[7] *See United States v. Lui Kin-Hong,* 83 F.3d 523 (1st Cir. 1996).

[8] *See Lui Kin-Hong v. United States,* 520 U.S. 1206 (1997).

[9] James Connolly, *'Stress' Plea Clears Viet Veteran in Drug Case,* at A10.

[10] *United States v. Kelly,* 519 F. Supp. 1029, 1031 (D. Mass. 1981).

[11] Richard Connolly, *'Gambling Must Be an Easy Job...,* BOS. GLOBE, Aug. 8, 1980.

[12] *See United States v. Zannino,* 895 F.2d 1 (1st Cir. 1990).

[13] NEW ENG. J. ON CRIM. & CIV. CONFINEMENT, Summer 1983.

[14] Bill Rolfe, *For a Judge, Sentencing Is No Easy Matter.*

[15] NEW ENG. J. ON CRIM. & CIV. CONFINEMENT, Summer 1983.

CHAPTER 12

The Personal Docket

In 1977, at the same time Joe Tauro was sitting as the judge in the *Rogers* case, he also became a litigant. His marriage of eighteen years was headed to divorce. On December 21, less than a week after the trial began, Tauro and his wife filed separate divorce actions on the same day. Both money and custody of the children were contested.

As the case proceeded, the parties agreed to a temporary custody arrangement whereby the children would remain in the family home, with the judge and his wife living there on alternate weeks. It was a tough divorce, and Tauro's efforts to keep his personal problems from affecting his job performance were not entirely successful.

> *Joe Tauro:* One day during all this George Higgins came to see me. He was a great friend of mine and also of my wife. He used to say that two of the nicest people he knew were Joe Tauro and Liz Tauro, and it's too bad they ever met. They never should have married. Higgins told me that day: "You're having trouble with the divorce. The assistant U.S. attorneys aren't causing the trouble. You're kicking them around unfairly, beating up on them in court and being extremely tough." He was letting me know that I was misbehaving as a judge. I had turmoil at home, and it was causing me to be unfair in the courtroom. You need somebody who you can trust to tell you something like that, and George was one of those people.

The divorce case came to a sad and abrupt end the following April, when Elizabeth Tauro died unexpectedly in her bed one night while Judge Tauro was vacationing at Disney World with the children.

Joe Tauro: She had congestive heart failure and died at a very young age. She had had illness problems, but this was out of the blue.

The divorce was tough, but it was a long time ago, and now I look back on her very fondly. Although we were not a good couple, she was a lovely person. It's a rare couple of weeks that goes by that I don't visit her grave and say a prayer. My wife June just recently planted a plant there.

Three years later, Tauro married Ann (June) Lefavour Jones, a physical therapist and ergonomics consultant with a B.A. from Simmons University, an M.S. from Emory, and an M.B.A. from Boston University.

Thirty years later, that marriage is going strong.

Joe and June Tauro on their wedding day, July 12, 1980

COURTESY OF HON. JOSEPH L. TAURO

Joe Tauro: June is the nicest, kindest, most wonderful person that God ever put on earth. She is very smart and very funny. I am so happy that when I go home at night I just stay with her. I never talk about what I do. Once in a while I'll tell her that there's a big story about me in the paper and she'll deflate me by saying: "There's always a big story about you in the paper."

The Next Generation

In the meantime, the fourth generation of American Tauros has grown and prospered. Orazio Tauro would be proud of his great-grandchildren. Joe Jr. is a graduate of the Culinary Institute of America, and had a successful career as a critically acclaimed chef before changing course and becoming an account executive with the Ipswich Shellfish Company.

Joe Tauro's daughter Beth followed in her father's footsteps, graduating from Brown University and Cornell Law School and becoming a lawyer. Beth changed directions too, and now is business development manager for the law firm of Edwards, Angell, Palmer & Dodge.

Son Chris also became a lawyer. He graduated from Boston University School of Law, which his grandfather attended. He is married to Claudia Venzal Tauro, and is now a partner at Edwards, Angell, Palmer & Dodge. Along the way, he served for four years as an assistant district attorney in Norfolk County, and later for four years as an assistant U.S. attorney in Boston.

Joe Jr. (left) and his brother Chris

COURTESY OF HON. JOSEPH L. TAURO

The Grandchildren

In Tauro's mind, however, the real stars of the next generation are his six grandchildren: Amanda, Jessica, Agustin, Elizabeth, Bridgette, and Emily. His office is a photographic gallery of their growth and progress. There is nothing Tauro enjoys more than a day at the beach with them, and later treating for ice cream. He may be a federal judge, but to them he is just "Gramps, the Ice Cream King."

Joe Tauro and his daughter Beth at her law school graduation

COURTESY OF HON. JOSEPH L. TAURO

Tauro's grandchildren, Summer 2010: Bridgette Tauro, Elizabeth Tauro, Agustin Groppa-Venzal, Jessica Saunders, Emily Tauro, Amanda Saunders.

COURTESY OF HON. JOSEPH L. TAURO

CHAPTER 13

Chief Judge, 1992-1999

When Joe Tauro came onto the federal court, its chief was Andrew Caffrey; then just a year into what would eventually become a fourteen-year tenure that ended only when health problems forced him to step down in 1986. Caffrey was an autocrat who ran the court as he saw fit, with little input from his colleagues. Under his administration, the court did not have regularly scheduled meetings, and on those occasions when an ad hoc meeting was called to make a decision on a matter, Caffrey frequently began the meeting by announcing that he had enough proxy votes to decide the matter in the way he wanted. The atmosphere on the court was strained.

> *Joe Tauro:* Drew Caffrey was very smart and hard working and he was always friendly to me, but in general he was not a cohesive influence on the court. We didn't communicate. Things happened without any real notice. We were very guarded with one another and did not discuss things frankly as a group. It was not uncommon for conflicting views to be planted with favored newspaper columnists.

Over time, however, as the court grew and changed, it became more difficult to control. In 1979 four new positions were created, and Robert Keaton, John McNaught, Rya Zobel (the court's first woman judge) and David Nelson (its first African-American judge) were appointed to fill them. Two more positions were added in 1985, filled by William Young and Mark Wolf.

Portrait of Andrew Caffrey

COURTESY OF THE U.S. DISTRICT COURT FOR THE DISTRICT OF MASSACHUSETTS

Both Joe and June Tauro made an early impression on Judge Wolf.

Mark Wolf: The first judicial conference I went to as a judge was in San Juan, Puerto Rico, in 1985. We had invited William Webster, the director of the FBI to the conference, which put us all in peril because the Department of Justice was then prosecuting in Connecticut some members of a Puerto Rican terrorist group. Having a big group of judges in Puerto Rico was a provocation, but bringing the director of the FBI to the conference was a big provocation. Everyone was on high alert. There were marshals on every floor, there were helicopters on the beach, and there was a lot of discussion about judicial security. The conference lasted for three days, and while we were there some Army officer on a motorbike was shot, apparently because we were there. The last day we had a big meeting and the marshals announced that they would be taking us all out to the airport in a motorcade. Later the motorcade took off, with sirens blaring, and the only judge who wasn't in the motorcade was Joe. He felt that the motorcade was just a sitting duck. He put on his shorts, and he and June took a taxi to the airport—he didn't want to look like a judge! Joe has a lot of common sense.

Mark Wolf

COURTESY OF THE U.S. DISTRICT COURT FOR THE DISTRICT OF MASSACHUSETTS

The judges' annual holiday that year was also memorable.

Mark Wolf: In those days the judges and their spouses sat around a long table at the Union Club, which wasn't as warm and jolly as it might have been. Suddenly Frank Murray keeled over. He was out, and here

William Young

COURTESY OF THE U.S. DISTRICT COURT FOR THE DISTRICT OF MASSACHUSETTS

> we were, all these presumably competent judges, just standing around with our mouths open. Joe's wife June is trained in the medical arts, so she ran to Frank and she did this, and she did that, and he came to, while the rest of us were being utterly ineffectual. Murray later told Joe that he thought he had died, and when he came to and opened his eyes, he was looking at an angel—June Tauro.

Since Tauro's appointment the court size had doubled, and many of the judges chafed at their exclusion from governance matters. In 1986, near the end of Caffrey's term, there was a breakthrough.

> *Joe Tauro:* A vacancy came up for a magistrate judge position. Those appointments are made by a vote of a majority of the district court judges. Under Caffrey's supervision a list of candidates was prepared and submitted to the court for the election. Caffrey's choice was Paul Healey, an assistant U.S. attorney, but Healey did not get a majority.
>
> I was one of several judges who favored Patti Saris, then chief of the Civil Division in the U.S. Attorney's Office. She wasn't on the list of candidates whose names Caffrey had submitted so we needed to get her on the ballot, so to speak. My instinct was to insist on a new slate. I mentioned this to Mark Wolf who, in typical fashion, did the research and came up with a rule that served to put Saris on the ballot. She won and became the new magistrate judge.

Patti Saris

COURTESY OF THE U.S. DISTRICT COURT FOR THE DISTRICT OF MASSACHUSETTS

Later that year, Chief Judge Caffrey announced that due to health problems he would be assuming senior status and stepping down as chief judge. Under a statute passed in 1982, his successor would be the senior sitting judge not over sixty-four years old, which was Frank Freedman, who had been commissioned on the same day as Joe Tauro, but Freedman had precedence because he was older. The new statute also established term limits: the chief judge could serve for only seven years, or until his or her seventieth birthday, whichever came first.

Seizing the opportunity, the judges of the court immediately insisted on changes in the way things were done.

Rya Zobel: We were at a judges' conference at the Balsams when we heard that Drew Caffrey was stepping down. We Massachusetts judges got together to talk about the new regime, and we made sure that the new chief, Frank Freedman, understood that we were going to participate. We put together rules of the court, which among other things called for monthly meetings. I suggested the first Tuesday of the month and everybody agreed. Judge Freedman, who was sitting in Springfield, wanted to be able to come only when he felt like it, but we insisted that he attend in person when he could and by speaker phone when he could not.

Rya Zobel

COURTESY OF THE U.S. DISTRICT COURT FOR THE DISTRICT OF MASSACHUSETTS

Judge Tauro was one of those advocating more democratic court governance.

Joe Tauro: Frank Freedman was a friendly and warm-hearted guy. He and I were very good friends, and I discussed the future with him. I told him we needed rules and meetings and a totally democratic process. I was the senior active judge in Boston, and it was important that he could trust me to run things when he wasn't around.

Frank Freedman

COURTESY OF THE U.S. DISTRICT COURT FOR THE DISTRICT OF MASSACHUSETTS

Rya Zobel: Before I came on the court, Frank Freedman and Joe Tauro had adjacent chambers in the old courthouse and shared a lobby together. Freedman sometimes would spend the night there on the sofa when he was in Boston because he didn't want to pay for a hotel room. The work of being the chief was not particularly congenial to him, and Joe was a friend and the next in line, so Joe had a big role.

Bill Young: Frank Freedman would preside, Oz-like, from the speaker phone. Joe was appropriately deferential to Frank and

> never stepped on Frank's toes, but for those of us in Boston—which was everyone but Frank— Joe was the go-to guy. He was the senior active judge, and he knew how things worked. So by the time he did become chief, although he had not been running things, people had been looking to him in an administrative sense.

The court changed a lot over the five years Freedman was chief judge, before he reached seventy and had to step down at the end of 1991.

> Joe Tauro: We had meetings, rules, and committees. The sun began to shine through. Our newer judges like Wolf, Woodlock, and Zobel zealously guarded the progress we had made. Every once in a while when Freedman would say there was no need for a monthly meeting, he would be shouted down, literally.

One of the changes Freedman made was to institute a series of three-judge committees to deal with various aspects of court business, such as probation, U.S. Attorney's Office, juries, and so on. It was part of the transition to democratic governance.

The Expense and Delay Reduction Plan

Another change that occurred during Judge Freedman's tenure was the development and implementation of the Expense and Delay Reduction Plan. The federal Civil Justice Reform Act (CJRA), passed in 1990, required each federal court to devise its own plan to improve case management and thus reduce the delay and expense of civil litigation in its district. Plans were to be submitted to Senator Joseph Biden, then chair of the Senate Judiciary Committee, which had drafted the CJRA. Each district chief judge was to appoint a committee to prepare the plan for its district. Chief Judge Freedman appointed Judges Tauro, Nelson, and Young as the members of that committee, with Tauro as its chair. The committee in turn appointed an advisory group to assist in the process, which included Magistrate Judges Lawrence Cohen and Michael Ponsor, Massachusetts Attorney General Scott Harshbarger, U.S. Attorney Wayne Budd, and a "who's who" of the Massachusetts bar.

> *Joe Tauro:* A lot of people felt that the essence of the Act was that Congress was stepping in and telling the courts how to run their business, which people resented. So the fundamental decision we had to make at the outset was whether or not we would cooperate. We figured it was better that we come up with the plan ourselves so that the lawyers and judges would be happy with it, rather than resist and have the Congress tell us what we would have to do.
>
> We held regular meetings, and periodically I would write Senator Biden and give him a progress report. They had sent general guidelines and empowered us to come up with our own specifics, which we did. I remember one member of the advisory group, Gael Mahoney, saying that the lawyers could live with whatever the rules might be, as long as they were the same for every courtroom. They wanted uniformity. We did that, and in the end we came up with a very good plan. That was because we had approached the job with a positive attitude.
>
> Later I was at a White House reception, which I think was at the time of Steve Breyer being sworn in to the Supreme Court, and I met Senator Biden there and introduced myself. He told me how pleased he was with the plan we had come up with.

The District Court for the District of Massachusetts adopted the Expense and Delay Reduction Plan on November 18, 1991, more than a year ahead of the deadline set by the CJRA. Major changes under the Plan included the following:

- automatic disclosure of certain documents and information without the need for lawyers to file document requests and interrogatories;
- an early case management conference with the judge assigned to the case (not a magistrate, as had been the common practice), which would set a schedule for the case;
- requiring attorneys to share estimates of the costs of litigation with clients early in the litigation; and
- recommending consideration of mediation or other alternative forms of dispute resolution.

Tauro had appointed Arthur Miller, the Harvard Law School professor who was a highly regarded expert in civil procedure, as the advisory group reporter.

Miller was one of those who was unenthusiastic at the start, but came to view the work of the advisory group as important. He credited the success to Tauro, whom he praised in a letter to the judge years later:

> *Arthur Miller:* I must confess, when you and Breyer ganged up on me to undertake the task, I did form the thought that, "Oh well, I guess there's nothing wrong with reinventing the wheel." But by the end of the experience, I had come to realize that I had just been given one of the greatest lessons in human engineering and dispute resolution ever seen in this hemisphere. As I watched you steer the document through successive waves of members of the bar, and then secure acquiescence from your colleagues, I came to the conclusion that I had witnessed a replay of the parting of the Dead Sea.

When he became chief judge, Tauro built on the changes that began under Freedman. The themes Tauro emphasized from the beginning were collegiality and democracy.

> *Joe Tauro:* My prime goal was to foster and enhance the spirit of collegiality in the court. I figured if I could achieve that, everything else would fall into place. I also wanted to spread responsibility for governance throughout the court, and in doing that, to make sure that credit for achievement was shared fully with those responsible.
>
> I made an auspicious beginning, coming down with the flu and being forced to miss my first meeting. I was touched by a message from Judge Zobel, who couldn't be present, but was writing to wish me well.

Changes were made in the court's monthly meetings. A formal agenda was prepared, and no proxies were permitted. Tauro ran the meetings strictly, discouraging whispering and requiring the judges to raise their hand to be called on. It injected an air of formality into the meetings, but made them more efficient and fairer. All the judges knew they would be called on to have their say, and that they would not be interrupted.

Michael Ponsor, Joe Tauro, and Edward Kennedy at Ponsor's swearing in as a federal judge in January 1994

COURTESY OF HON. JOSEPH L. TAURO

> *Michael Ponsor:* Judge Tauro is a guy who knows how to run a meeting. He does not speak to the issues himself unless it is something he really feels strongly about. He makes sure others have a chance to speak. He moves the meetings along and gets things done. He brought the boulders to our attention and didn't let us get bogged down in gravel. What I remember was an absence of controversy: things just moved.

> *Ted Harrington:* He was a great leader. Because of his political skills, he was able to bring divergent views together and get things done without leaving any hostility. We are a diverse group, and Joe was very important in bringing us together.

In addition to the regular monthly meetings on the first Tuesday of each month, the court had regular informal monthly luncheon meetings. It took a while to get everyone to participate, but those meetings became and have continued to be an important means of fostering collegiality and cohesiveness in the court.

Tauro also initiated some small changes to the court's holiday dinner. He abandoned the long thirty-person table in favor of round tables seating eight or ten, and he juggled the seating arrangements every year. And he added the Toast to the Court.

> *Rya Zobel:* One judge is designated every year to present the toast to the court. It has taken some interesting forms. When I did it, I gave a citation to each one of my colleagues similar to a citation in a Harvard honorary degree, which was great fun to do. It's a lot of work, but it goes over well.

> *Doug Woodlock:* He understood the importance of collegiality. I think that had to do with his father having been the Chief Justice of the Supreme Judicial Court. The idea is that you are herding cats or transporting bullfrogs in a wheelbarrow—this may be a group of prima donnas, but it is important to maintain the collegiality of it. Joe worked really hard at doing that. For instance, where he might have felt slights before, he let those pass. We all felt like we were equals, working together for the greater good of the order. The phrase he always used was that he was an equal among firsts. He was very good at knitting the court together.

> *Rick Stearns:* A lot of the power that other judges might have wanted to arrogate to themselves he willingly delegated to others. It was a style of leadership based on a true opportunity to talk things through. He would never overrule majority sentiment.

> *Bill Young:* He loves the court and because he loves the court, he loves all those who love the court. And it is not just this court, but really the institution, broadly. There are two stories that illustrate this point.

One is about the time when we were at the old courthouse. The Suffolk sessions at the Massachusetts Superior Court had been forced out of the courthouse in Pemberton Square to be squeezed into state government offices elsewhere. They didn't have enough space for their sessions, and they didn't have money to rent. We on the federal court discussed accommodating some Superior Court sessions in our court because we had more courtrooms than judges. The discussion was high-minded and theoretical. It ended when Joe said: "I'll give them my courtroom." He wasn't kidding. He gave up his courtroom and moved into a little room like a closet—boom—just like that. They remember that, and to this day, I believe he is the only person invited to their annual dinner who is not a past or present judge of the Superior Court. Joe just loves the institution in everything he does, and if you pan it, he is angry.

The second story is one Joe tells about his father's swearing in as chief justice of the Massachusetts SJC. The prior chief was Ray Wilkins, a magnificent man for whom I had clerked. Justice Wilkins stepped down because of poor health. He was very frail and had lost a leg to an embolism. His background was old Boston, very different from Tauro's father, who had been appointed by Governor Sargent. Nonetheless, Wilkins made it to the ceremony with the aid of a walker, to swear in Tauro Sr. This was an act which both Tauro Sr. and Joe appreciated, and it was a story Joe told to illustrate loyalty to the institution. It was a perfect Joe story because it built me up, since I had clerked for Wilkins, and it built up the institution of the court.

Raymond S. Wilkins, G. Joseph Tauro, and Frank Sargent at Tauro's swearing in as Chief Justice of the SJC

COURTESY OF HON. JOSEPH L. TAURO

The three-judge committees instituted under Freedman were a step toward democracy, but Tauro felt they were inefficient. Instead, he favored a system of single-liaison judges who took over the responsibilities of the committees. The liaison judges had responsibility for oversight of his or her section on a daily basis and reported to the full court at its monthly meetings. This led to greater responsiveness, and gave each judge real court governance responsibility. In contemplating this change, Tauro turned to his rules guru, Judge Woodlock.

> *Joe Tauro:* I ran the idea by Doug Woodlock, who thought it made sense and who supported the change when I proposed it. It was the first of many occasions when I turned to him for such advice and support during my years as chief. Typically I would call him at 8:00 in the morning. At that hour, he was in the office, while I'd be at home, having coffee.

Tauro tried to put the other judges in charge of tasks for which they were suited and then support their efforts. It was a management approach that went over well with his colleagues and worked well for the court as an institution.

> *Doug Woodlock:* Joe was and is probably the most effective executive I have ever seen. He knows how to delegate, and he knows how to get the people to whom he has delegated to do things for him. He is never going to get deeply involved in micro-managing. He expects people to get stuff done.

> *Rya Zobel:* The liaison-judge system that Joe put in has worked well. For me, I was the jury person, which was a very good experience. I was able to get the statute changed so that we began using the state lists of prospective jurors, which were a lot broader than the voting records we had been using. Also, we had been having grand jury problems because the U.S. attorney was impaneling twelve, thirteen, or fourteen grand juries. They would bring them in and then they wouldn't have any business for them. We cut down on the number of grand juries, and we went to a one-day, one-trial system for regular juries, which made jury service less onerous and fairer.
>
> Later when Bill Young was chief judge, Judge Lindsay became the jury person and he did a great job of getting the system improved and the jury pool made even more

> representative. The problem we have always had is that people are not particularly stable in their residences in Roxbury and some of the Black areas of town, both here and elsewhere. Many are not citizens and a lot of mail is never delivered to them and comes back. Lindsay got the system changed so that now if we get mail returned from somebody in Roxbury we can send to the same zip code again in order to get a more responsive jury. That is the kind of thing a liaison judge can do and an example of the way the system has worked.

Steps were also taken to open up criminal defense appointments, an area where Judge Wolf served as the liaison judge. The existing system was largely an "old boys' network" where most of the appointments went to a small group of attorneys who were former assistant U.S. attorneys. The new system ensured that criminal defense appointments would be spread out among a much larger group of attorneys, including women, minorities, and younger lawyers.

The New Courthouse

The biggest change during Judge Tauro's tenure was the courthouse itself. In 1998, the last full year of Tauro's term as chief judge, the court moved to the new John Joseph Moakley Courthouse on Fan Pier. The Moakley Courthouse houses the District Court, the First Circuit Court of Appeals, the U.S. Attorney's offices, extensive facilities for the U.S. Marshals Service, the pretrial and probation services, a cafeteria, and a daycare center. It is an impressive building, which has won numerous design awards, including one from the National Endowment for the Arts and one from the American Institute of Architects.

The origins of the project date back to the 1980s, as a growing federal court faced the problem of what to do about its outdated facilities at the McCormack Post Office and Courthouse Building in Boston's Post Office Square. There were two schools of thought among the judges: those who argued for a new courthouse, and those who felt that a new courthouse was unrealistic and that the court should instead press for a complete renovation of the existing facility. Chief Judge Levin Campbell was in the latter camp. Campbell felt that a campaign for a new courthouse would likely fail and lead to the court getting nothing and that a floor-to-ceiling renovation of the existing facility was the best achievable result.

Tauro was among the minority pushing for a new facility. There was no suggestion that the court could move its business elsewhere while renovations took place, and Tauro felt the court could not function effectively during the two years or so that renovations were expected to take. Among other things, significant portions of the elevator service would be out of commission, and even at full capacity, elevator service was notoriously inadequate. The famous episode of Judge Walter Skinner sentencing one criminal defendant to the time spent in the elevator getting to court was one example of just how bad it was.

> *Joe Tauro:* I kept saying no to repairing the old building. I just refused to go along with it. I was concerned that the District Court with its enormous traffic flow of jurors, witnesses, lawyers, and parties could not handle the business of the court during a major renovation. The Circuit Court, although busy, did not have the same volume of traffic.

> *Doug Woodlock:* He was kind of a voice crying in the wilderness for getting out of Post Office Square.

Tauro's adamant position in favor of a new courthouse can be traced in part to some advice Judge Frank Murray gave Tauro about his own courtroom when he came on the bench.

> *Joe Tauro:* Murray told me: don't make do with your courtroom. I was supposed to have the courtroom of Lee Campbell, who was going to the Court of Appeals. Everybody wanted me to move in there, but the courtroom was only half renovated. Frank Murray said: "Don't ever do that. If you do, as long as you live as a judge of this court, that's the way it will be. Refuse to go any place until it is finished." He was right. If I had done what they said, I'd still be sitting there.

One of Tauro's allies in pressing for a new federal courthouse was Justice Stephen Breyer, who was then sitting on the First Circuit Court of Appeals and in line to be its next chief. Breyer's chambers were directly across from Tauro's in

Douglas Woodlock, Stephen Breyer, Sandra Lynch and Joe Tauro on the day the Moakley Courthouse was dedicated.

COURTESY OF HON. JOSEPH L. TAURO

the McCormack Courthouse, and the two men were friends. Breyer played a pivotal role in opposing a proposal that would have moved the First Circuit into the O'Neill Building on Causeway Street, thus opening up more space for the federal District Court in the McCormack Building. He felt strongly that the First Circuit Court of Appeals and the District Court should sit and have their chambers in the same building in order to foster good relations between the two courts. Breyer became a proponent of building a new courthouse to house both courts.

Another ally, and the man to whom Tauro would ultimately delegate a leading role in the building of the courthouse, was his colleague, Doug Woodlock, then the most junior judge. Woodlock was an early advocate for a new courthouse.

> *Doug Woodlock:* I was the low man on the totem pole, so I had an office on the fourth floor of the McCormack Building that had been a Social Security office, or something like that, so that gives you some idea. Most of the judges were of the view that there would never be a new courthouse, but if the two youngest guys on each court, Breyer and I, wanted to give it a try that was fine with them. Judge Campbell put me on the Space and Facilities Committee for the Judicial

> Conference, which was where the issues were being discussed at that time, in the late 1980s. Joe was not yet the chief of our court—Freedman was—and there was a period of time when I was functioning as a sort of minister without portfolio.

Woodlock forged an alliance with an unlikely partner, veteran democratic congressman Joe Early from Worcester. Early was an important member on the House Appropriations Committee.

> *Doug Woodlock:* Joe Early had opposed my nomination for the federal court because he wanted someone from the Worcester area. The statute authorized the federal court to hold court in Worcester, among some other cities, but there was no judge sitting in Worcester, and Early was not happy about it. He had called Kennedy to oppose my nomination.
>
> After I was confirmed I was advised to pay a visit to Early. I went out to Worcester to see him and Early said to me: "Where are you from?"
>
> I said I was from Ipswich.
>
> "That's what I thought," he said, "Cape Cod."
>
> I said: "Well, it's really not Cape Cod, it's Cape Ann."
>
> He said: "Cape Cod, Cape Ann, I don't give a good God damn. You're not from Worcester County! Nothing personal," he said, "but I opposed you for that."
>
> Then he said he wanted to show me their courthouse. They had this really nice courthouse. He told me: "There should be a judge out here. Worcester is the largest city in New England that doesn't have a federal judge." He had a good argument and I agreed with him that we should do something. Bill Young felt the same way and we started pushing the idea of having a Worcester session.
>
> After that, we took the position that there should be a fully renovated and expanded courthouse in Worcester. Early said: "By the way, there should be a new courthouse in Boston." We said that would be good. Then while I was working on the Worcester thing I got a call from the administrative office of the U.S. courts saying that there was supposed to be a study of a new courthouse in Boston. That was news to me. It was an earmark in the Appropriations Bill. That was Early. Early drew Congressman Moakley into it.

Moakley was the dean of the Massachusetts delegation and very close to Early, and he became very helpful to us.

Stephen Breyer: Moakley's role was critical when the time finally came to get the appropriations voted, at the point later where we had an architect and a site and we had a real number that we needed to get the courthouse built, which was something like $220 million. The original House appropriation vote had been for only $57 million, I think, but with the help of Senator Kennedy's office we managed to convince the Senate to vote $183 million or so. The appropriation then went to the House-Senate conference committee, where it was expected that the Senate was going to recede to the House and the House's much lower number would prevail. However, Early, instead of sending a staffer to the conference committee meeting or attending himself, persuaded Moakley to go. Moakley was the chairman of the House Rules Committee and a powerful presence in the House. When the courthouse appropriations item was raised, a Senate staffer said: "The Senate recedes to the House," but Moakley immediately called out: "No it doesn't!"

That is how we got the $180 million approved, but we still needed to figure out how to get the rest of the money we needed. We wrote a letter to the U.S. attorney saying we're terribly sorry but we won't have space for you in the new courthouse because we need to scale it back due to a shortage of funds. That led the U.S. attorney to enlist the help of the U. S. Attorney General, Bill Barr, who took the position that the money was necessary because the U.S. Attorney's Office had to be in the courthouse for reasons of security. This was a valid point, and Congress appropriated the money we needed. In the end the project was brought in on time and on budget, and the cost on a per-square-foot basis was right at the average of other comparable new court construction. The result was a very nice courthouse that was much needed.

Politics on the federal level was only one side of the equation, however. There was also local politics to deal with. Here Judge Tauro played a pivotal role.

> *Joe Tauro:* I was presiding over a naturalization ceremony at Faneuil Hall with Mayor Flynn serving as the speaker. After the ceremony, I asked Flynn if he had a few minutes to chat. I told him about our chronic courthouse problems, including the inadequacy of the facilities and the lack of security for those required to come before the court, either as parties, witnesses, or jurors. I shared my opinion that the inadequacy of the court facilities was a negative reflection on the city itself. I told him that we needed a new courthouse, but that we just didn't know how to get such a major project out of the garage and onto the tracks.
>
> I asked him point blank if he could and would help us get a new courthouse building. He replied by asking me: "Where do you want the building to go?"
>
> I answered: "Any place you want it to go where it would most benefit the city."
>
> Flynn told me he would have one of his staff get in touch with me. That happened within a half hour of my returning to the office.

At one point early in his career, Flynn had been a probation officer for the Superior Court for Tauro's father, and he had a very good relationship with the son. It was a relationship that benefited the project throughout.

> *Doug Woodlock:* Through Joe we had everything we could ask for from the Mayor and his office. My view was that if the Boston Redevelopment Authority got involved we would spend endless amounts of time talking to them and negotiating with them and we would be better off cutting them out. This is one place Joe came in. He called up and asked Flynn to talk to the people who deal with this kind of thing. We were asked what we wanted and I said we wanted a development person on the Mayor's staff with whom we could deal instead of a bunch of people at the B.R.A. That person turned out to be John Connolly, the Mayor's development person, who is a terrific guy. So we dealt with John Connolly, and if the B.R.A. needed to be talked to Connolly did it. Every time we went into the Mayor's office, the first question was always "How's Joe?"

The site requirements were three to four acres, within a half mile of City Hall. There were four possibilities: (1) a site near North Station where a Stop & Shop had been; (2) a site at the intersection of New Chardon and Merrimac Streets, where the Brooke Courthouse has since been built; (3) the site next to Boston Common where the new Ritz Carlton Hotel is now situated; and (4) the present site on Fan Pier.

The Fan Pier site was then owned by well-known restaurateur, Anthony Athanas. In the late 1980s Athanas and his Fan Pier development partners, the Pritzkers of Chicago, had sued each other in what became a bitter litigation for extremely high stakes. Athanas lost badly in the trial court and appealed. The extent of the judgment—$59 million plus many millions more in pre- and post-judgment interest—threatened to ruin Athanas financially and force him into bankruptcy. His major asset was Fan Pier, and his financial troubles brought Fan Pier into play as a potentially viable site for the federal court.

> *Doug Woodlock:* Anthony had all this land and no cash and a big judgment he had to settle. We did a study, organized by the B.R.A. and the G.S.A., which showed that this was the least expensive place per square foot of any of the four sites we had been thinking of. We talked to the Pritzkers, the B.R.A. talked to the Pritzkers, and Joe Moakley and Joe Early talked to Anthony and said: "You ought to sell this thing."

The site selection was put to a vote of the District Court during the last year of Frank Freedman's term as chief judge. A clear majority favored the Fan Pier site. Joe Tauro was one of those who did not. When the vote was over, however, there was no looking back and no recriminations.

> *Bill Young:* When there are differences of opinion and a matter is decided by majority vote, frequently there may be echoes, not in a formal parliamentary sense of 'I want it reconsidered,' but you can get, "Well, we should have done it this way, but because we didn't do that. . ." Joe isn't like that. Once it's done, it's done. That's the way he is and that's the way this was.

In the early summer of 1991, the General Services Administration announced the purchase of a 4.6 acre parcel on Fan Pier from Anthony Athanas for $34 million. Since the appeal of the Athanas-Pritzker litigation was still pending, the money was placed in escrow until the appeal was resolved. That happened in December 1991, when the Supreme Judicial Court denied Athanas's appeal, which meant that the $34 million he was paid for the site went to the Pritzkers as part of what they were owed.

Shortly after the Supreme Judicial Court handed down its decision, Judge Tauro began his term as chief judge. During that term, the courthouse was designed and built, and plans were put in place for the underground extension of the MBTA Silver Line, which would extend public transportation from South Station to the courthouse. It was done in Tauro's signature style: delegate and support. Principal day-to-day responsibility remained with Judges Woodlock and Breyer. When the situation called for it, Tauro would use his bully pulpit as chief to advocate for and defend the project.

> *Rya Zobel:* Judge Woodlock was the prime mover, but Joe facilitated it. He was a fantastic cheerleader for the project.

The John Joseph Moakley Courthouse, at its completion in 1998

PHOTOGRAPHER: DAVID RYAN. PRINTED WITH PERMISSION OF *THE BOSTON GLOBE*/GETTY IMAGES.

> *Bill Young:* When Senator McCain was after us for the expense of the big glass wall that is the hallmark of the new courthouse, and Joe was asked about it on nationwide television, he answered: "We don't hold the sessions of this court in a Quonset hut." We his colleagues loved that. He was saying: "Get off my back. This is a U.S. federal courthouse."

When the courthouse was completed during the last year of Tauro's tenure as chief, he was now the senior active judge and thus had first choice of courtroom and chambers. It didn't do him much good, however, as the judges' chambers had been carefully designed to contain identical square footages and amenities. As with Tauro's entire tenure, the focus had been on bringing the court together.

Stephen Breyer's Appointment to the Supreme Court

During Tauro's years as chief judge, another event in which Tauro played an important supporting role was the appointment of Judge Stephen Breyer to the U.S. Supreme Court in 1994. Breyer and Tauro had long been close friends. It was a relationship that started when they had chambers across the hall from each other in the old courthouse, and flourished as they worked together over the years on issues of mutual interest like the move to the new courthouse and the battles over judicial compensation. When a position on the U.S. Supreme Court opened in 1993, Judge Breyer was on the short list of those considered, along with Ruth Bader Ginsburg and some others. Breyer's candidacy, however, was a casualty of Massachusetts driving.

> *Stephen Breyer:* I was biking home from work and as I made a turn near my home I was hit by a car. The next thing I knew I was in an ambulance. I broke a rib and the rib went into my lung. The lung was partially collapsed and they put a tube in. I was in the hospital for a few days and while I was there a small delegation from the White House, including Vince Foster, came up to interview me in connection with the U.S. Supreme Court opening. They had taken the tube out and I was getting better when I got a call from Senator Kennedy telling me that I needed to get down to Washington to meet with the President.

The doctors told me I couldn't fly, so I had my son-in-law drive Joanna and me to New York and from there we took the train to Washington where I had lunch with President Clinton.

Breyer was taking strong medication for his injuries, and was hardly at his best. After lunch, Clinton apparently said something like, "Well, I understand he's very bright but he was just very dull at the lunch." The job went to Ruth Bader Ginsburg, a disappointment to Breyer which he handled with grace, expressing his appreciation for the process and the honor of being considered and his support for Ginsburg.

The following year Clinton found himself with another opening to fill, and before that happened, some of Breyer's friends had made sure that the White House and the President were aware of the back story to his earlier lunch with Breyer. One friend was Joe Tauro.

Joe Tauro: I wrote President Clinton a letter saying that when he interviewed Breyer the first time it was just after Breyer had been hit by a car, and he had a rib sticking into his lungs, so naturally it was not a good interview. I said he owed it to himself to give Breyer another look if the opportunity arose.

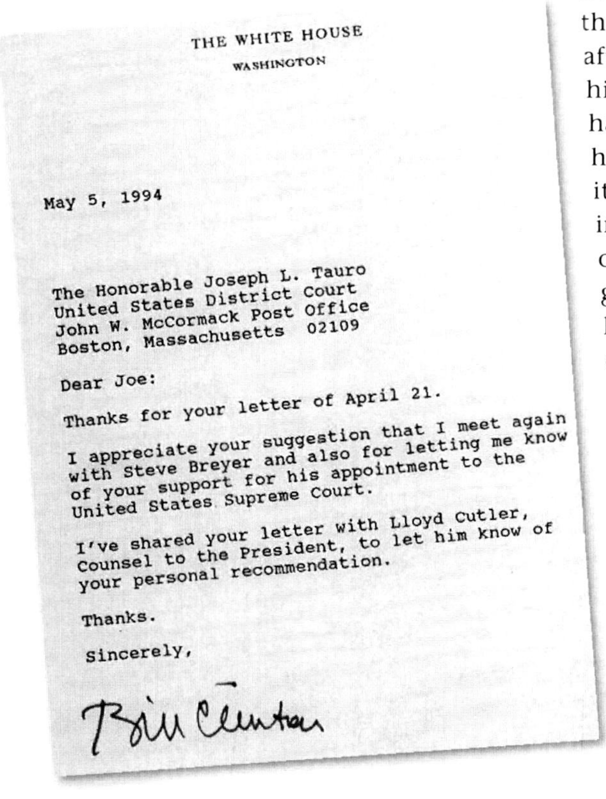

THE WHITE HOUSE
WASHINGTON

May 5, 1994

The Honorable Joseph L. Tauro
United States District Court
John W. McCormack Post Office
Boston, Massachusetts 02109

Dear Joe:

Thanks for your letter of April 21.

I appreciate your suggestion that I meet again with Steve Breyer and also for letting me know of your support for his appointment to the United States Supreme Court.

I've shared your letter with Lloyd Cutler, Counsel to the President, to let him know of your personal recommendation.

Thanks.

Sincerely,

Bill Clinton

President Clinton's response to Joe Tauro's letter recommending Stephen Breyer for the U.S. Supreme Court

COURTESY OF HON. JOSEPH L. TAURO

It wasn't long before that opportunity did arise, and this time Breyer got the appointment.

> *Mike Mone:* In the spring of 1994 a second Supreme Court opening came up when Justice Harry Blackmun retired. At that point I was a regent in the American College of Trial Lawyers. Judge Tauro called me to ask if I could get the College to endorse Breyer, but I told him that the College didn't endorse candidates for court. However, not long after that I went out to a meeting of the College in Arizona, and Breyer spoke at that meeting. He gave a terrific speech, which was substantive, engaging, funny–everything you could want in twenty-five minutes.

> *Joe Tauro:* Mike Mone called me after the meeting to say that Breyer had given a really good speech. I learned that there was a video of the speech, and I asked Mike if he could get it. Within an hour or two I had it, and Breyer was just as good as Mike had described him: brilliant, witty and everything he hadn't been at the lunch with Clinton. I knew that Judge Stearns had been a Rhodes Scholar with Clinton and was a friend of his, so I brought this up with him and asked him if he would take a look at the video, and if he thought it was as good as I did, would he get the video to Clinton and ask him to take a look at it. Rick discussed it with his wife Patty and then did just that.

> *Rick Stearns:* Bill Clinton and I had roomed together for a term at Oxford, and we had traveled a lot in Europe together. We were very close. At the time Judge Breyer was being considered for the first Supreme Court opening, I was asked by the President what I thought of Steve Breyer. I gave him a glowing review. Then after the interview, the President called me to say that he hadn't been able to get anywhere with Breyer at the lunch. He found him a cold fish. It puzzled me until I found out later about the bike accident.
>
> Then when the second opening was pending, Joe Tauro asked me to take a look at the tape of Breyer speaking at the

> lawyers' meeting. In it he was witty, affable, funny—just the way I know him to be. I passed the tape on to a good friend in the White House, and asked him to get the President to look at it for a minute. "Just start anywhere, and if he doesn't like it after sixty seconds, stop watching." I was betting he would keep watching, and he did.

Not long after that, Clinton announced he had chosen Breyer to be the next Supreme Court justice.

Judge David Nelson

Not every episode concluded as happily as the courthouse move and the Breyer appointment, and not every duty of the chief could be delegated. For Tauro, one of those occurred when his colleague and close friend, David Nelson, became afflicted with Alzheimer's disease. As the disease progressed, Judge Nelson began to fall farther and farther behind in his cases. The handling of Judge Nelson's situation was left to the discretion of the Chief.

> *Joe Tauro:* I went to David. I took Breyer along with me so there would be someone else there. I told David that what I wanted to do was to take his cases away from him so that I could divide them among the other judges to give them a chance to deal with these cases, and I would give David fifty brand-new cases that were not behind on anything. That would allow him to start from scratch, with a greatly reduced caseload, and not feel so pressed to catch up. He said: "I'm trusting you to do what you say you're going to do."
>
> I answered him: "Did you ever feel you could not trust me?"
>
> He said: "No, never."
>
> It was difficult to have that conversation with him, but he had slipped enough that we had to make some arrangement.
>
> My colleagues gave me a lot of leeway. I reported to them and they all thought what I had suggested was a good idea and agreed with it.

Judge Nelson assumed senior status on September 27, 1991, and died in 1998.

Friendships with Colleagues

One of the ingredients to Tauro's success as chief judge, as it has been in so much of what he accomplished in his career, was his ability to make strong and sustained friendships. He cared about people, and he found lots of ways of showing it.

> *Rya Zobel:* When I first came on board as a district court judge in 1979, Joe and I shared a lobby. It was really very funny because I was certainly inexperienced and he was certainly experienced, but he had no compunction about telling me how to do my business! I have a friend who talks about "UPG"—unsolicited parental guidance—and Joe was full of UPG for me. He'd tell me how to settle cases, he'd tell me what I should say to the lawyers. We'd meet in the lobby and talk during recesses or before we went to court in the morning and there wasn't a meeting where he didn't have a bit of advice for me. Sometimes I would follow it and sometimes I would say yes and do it my way, but he is a very shrewd person and he has a political sense like few people do, and it would have been foolish of me to ignore what he had to say. It was a beautiful and sweet relationship which had a kind of paternal quality.

> *Sandy Lynch:* When I was appointed as a judge of the First Circuit in 1995, my chambers were across from Joe's in the old building. He was enormously kind to me. He would bring me over for coffee. He would explain things to me. If there was a visiting dignitary such as a Congressman, he would be sure to invite me over. And if there was a District Court event of any significance, Joe would make sure that I was included.

Sandra Lynch

COURTESY OF HON. SANDRA LYNCH

> *Rick Stearns:* When I first began on the court, all I remembered were all the confrontations we had had, not on a personal

> level but on an institutional level, when I was a prosecutor in the U.S. Attorney's Office and he was a judge. In the U.S. Attorney's Office, he was regarded as the most lenient judge on the court. He was unfailingly polite with the prosecutors, but determined to get his way, and there could be some tense moments between the assistant U.S. attorney and Judge Tauro. I never would have predicted, when I was appointed to this court, that he would become virtually my best friend on the court.

Tauro was also somebody to whom a lot of people came for advice because they valued his wisdom and trust him.

> *Nancy Gertner:* I was appointed to the bench by President Clinton early in his first term, and although the Democrats were still in control, I had handled abortion cases and other controversial matters, and my confirmation wasn't a given. I got through the Judiciary Committee in November 1993, but then at some point all of a sudden I got a call from Lloyd Cutler, White House counsel. It had to do with the forms that criminal defense attorneys were required to fill out identifying the source of cash they receive. When I received cash from a client, particularly in the midst of representation, I would refuse to disclose the source on the grounds of attorney-client privilege. I would write that on the form and tell the government that if they wanted the information, they would have to go to court and litigate it and get a ruling requiring disclosure. I had opinions from both the Massachusetts Bar Association and the American Bar Association backing me up in this approach. Many criminal defense attorneys did this.
>
> As it happened, in the middle of the confirmation process, the Department of Justice decided to come after us. Ultimately, someone in the White House pulled them back, and I got confirmed, but then before my swearing-in, the matter resurfaced. Cutler called me and told me that the President wanted me to postpone my swearing in. I said no. Then I got a call back from Cutler saying that if there was any negative publicity about the way I had filled out these forms, I should agree to disqualify myself from any case involving the government, which is a lot of what a federal judge hears. I was

scared. This was 1994, and the landscape was littered with judicial appointments and other appointments whom Clinton didn't stand up for. I decided to go talk to Joe about it.

I had liked and respected Joe Tauro as a judge, and I trusted him. I trusted his political sense, I trusted his courage, I trusted that he cared about the same things I cared about, and I trusted that he would take a principled position. I can't quote actually what he said, because the language was not for quotation, but he told me to tell Cutler off in no uncertain terms. He was telling me I was right and should stand up to them. "Tell them to talk to me," he said at one point. "Judges get sued all the time; it doesn't mean anything." It was such a fabulous conversation.

When I did tell Cutler no, he said to me that if there was any negative publicity about the forms, I could be investigated and find myself the first federal judge to be impeached before being sworn in. But I stuck with my position and that didn't happen.

Joyce Alexander: Before I came on the bench I had heard of Judge Tauro through my father, who used to speak admiringly about the Tauro family, and their sense of pride and who they were. So when I became a magistrate judge, he was one of the people I went to see. He became a friend, a confidante, and an advisor to me. He had intellectual acumen, integrity, and character, and a sense of humanity that is rare. He respects people and has a love of people. He has all of the characteristics you would want in a judge. Being the only African-American woman on the bench, there were times when I needed to talk to someone to get a perspective about something someone said or did, and Joe was someone I could talk to. He was very well respected in the African-American community both here and nationally. For me, I always felt at home with him and I could talk to him about things I couldn't talk to very many people about.

Joyce Alexander

COURTESY OF THE U.S. DISTRICT COURT FOR THE DISTRICT OF MASSACHUSETTS

When I became chief magistrate judge, Joe was the chief judge of the District Court. I told him that my family would be coming from out of town for the swearing in. Joe was so proud. He said: "We have to do this right!" It turned out to be a beautiful ceremony, with people coming in from all over the country. Joe gave a terrific speech. It wasn't about that I was a nice person; he talked about my credentials and why I should be a chief. He talked about my ability to decide cases and the fact that I was rarely reversed. He was wonderful. In the end, I stayed on the bench for thirty years. I don't know if I would have stayed if I hadn't had Joe.

The warm face that Joe Tauro had for his colleagues was the same for everyone.

Tim Webster: One of the things I took away from my year of clerking for the judge was to treat everybody really nicely. He had a genuineness that was manifest not just in the courtroom but throughout the building. When the janitorial staff came around, it was: "Hi Elizabeth, Hi Sean. How are you doing?" Then when Judge Stearns walked by in the corridor it was: "Hi Judge, how are you doing?" There was a real kindness that is not part of the stereotypical image of a life-appointed federal judge. It was very educational for me and my co-clerk.

Joe Tauro and one of his clerks, Tim Webster, 2008

COURTESY OF HON. JOSEPH L. TAURO

CHAPTER 14

Community Service

Among many innovations during Tauro's tenure as chief judge was the initiation of periodic seminars at which the entire court, or most of it, would sit on the panel and respond to topics and questions raised by the Bar.

> *Joe Tauro:* At the time we started it, I don't think there was another court in the country that did it, and certainly not a federal court that had the entire bench there answering any questions the Bar wanted to put to them. We decided to do that as a way of sharing our information and experience. But it allowed us to learn as well, from their questions and comments. So it was a two-way street. I thought that was typical of the attitude that caused so many of our judges to teach. I think we have a generous attitude about sharing our experiences with the constituencies.

Tauro taught trial advocacy at Boston University for twenty-five years. He has also taught seminars or given lectures at Harvard, Suffolk, and Brown.

> *Joe Tauro:* I enjoy teaching very much. I stopped only because I got tired. I had twenty or so in a class for twenty-five years, so I taught about 500 young lawyers. I run into them all the time. I'll be at a cocktail party, and some young woman will come up to me and say she was in my class. They are always very appreciative. One thing I would tell them is that the most important thing a young lawyer can develop is a rubber ass. You're going to get knocked on your ass plenty and the question is: Do you lay there, or do you bounce back up?

> There is no place where you need the capacity to bounce back up more than at a trial.

In addition to his years of teaching, Judge Tauro served for many years as a trustee of the Children's Hospital Medical Center in Boston, as well as of the Massachusetts General Hospital. He currently serves as a trustee emeritus and a member of the Brown University Corporation. He was a member of the Judicial Conference of the United States, and served on the Judicial Conference Committee on Codes of Conduct, as well as its Committee on the Jury System.

Tauro has been recognized many times for his contributions to the community, both on and off the bench. His many awards and degrees include: the Massachusetts Bar Association's Hennessy Leadership Award, and the Boston Bar Association's Citation of Judicial Excellence.

He has received honorary degrees from a host of institutions, including Brown University, Boston University, Northeastern University, Suffolk University, the University of Massachusetts, and the New England School of Law. Brown University gave Tauro its Brown Bear Award, and the Cornell Law School faculty gave him its Distinguished Alumnus Award.

Earle Cooley, Chairman of the Board of Boston University (at left) as Joe Tauro receives an honorary degree from Boston University President Jon Westling.

COURTESY OF HON. JOSEPH L. TAURO

CHAPTER 15

The Fernald School Revisited

In 1999, Judge Tauro stepped down at the end of his term as chief and resumed his role as a rank-and-file member of the court, albeit its most senior member. He was still going strong.

One of the cases he was still dealing with was the Fernald School litigation. The judge closed all the mental health litigations in 1994 and technically he never reopened them, but they didn't all go away. Beryl Cohen brought a lengthy motion to reopen in 2004, which Tauro denied without prejudice, but there were consent decrees in place, and the judge remained on call when controversies relating to them surfaced.

Fernald became the biggest issue. It had been closed to new admissions since 1993, and its population had shrunk radically due to community placements, transfers, and deaths. Anxious to save the huge amounts of money required to keep it open, and to seek alternative uses for its large campus, the state pushed to close Fernald. Some of the Fernald families felt otherwise. This battle continues.

> *Joe Tauro:* Now I have this big battle over the last 150 residents. They want to stay there, or at least they want the opportunity to stay there. Governor Romney and now Governor Patrick have taken the position that they can't stay there—it has to be sold. But it's just a handful of profoundly sick people, and where are they going to go? I tell them: carve out a little place for them. You can sell the rest of the place and make plenty of dough on this. Give them a chance to die. That's the battle now [in 2009]. I issued an order saying that if they could find these people a place that's as good for them as

Fernald, then they could transfer them, but they just can't arbitrarily eliminate Fernald as a choice.

What I did was appoint the U.S. Attorney, Michael Sullivan, to be the court monitor for Fernald. He and his assistant, Ray Farqhuar, spent a year coming up with a report. I directed that there could be no further transfers from Fernald until I had the report, and I told Sullivan to take his time and do a thorough job. When he issued his report I then made my decision that they had to give people a choice, which meant letting them stay at Fernald if they wanted to, because Sullivan had concluded that any other place they might send them would not meet the requirement of being as good or better than Fernald.

Beryl Cohen: There are 200 employees, more or less, at Fernald today, providing services to a couple of hundred people. These employees range from people who change diapers, to LPNs, RNs, and people who do training and education. It is a whole complex of professional and direct-care staff for the individuals who are there, and that doesn't happen out in the community. What Judge Tauro has done is to provide the option.

In ruling on the motion to close Fernald, Judge Tauro continued to approach the case as he had from the start, paying little attention to the state's jurisdictional defenses and focusing entirely on what he felt was right for Fernald residents and their families. Tim Webster was one of Tauro's clerks at the time.

Tim Webster: There was a legal issue that I think concerned whether the court had jurisdiction, but the judge was not particularly concerned about the legal niceties of the case. He felt he had a special duty to the parents and residents of Fernald.

Joe Tauro: From the beginning of the case until thirty-five years later, the state has always taken the position that I don't have jurisdiction. Jurisdiction has never been a particular

> fascination of mine. We've done an awful lot for a case in which scholars might question jurisdiction!

In the end, the Commonwealth did finally prevail in its court battle over closing Fernald. On appeal of Judge Tauro's order, the First Circuit Court of Appeals ruled that shutdown plans could continue, and in April 2009 the U.S. Supreme Court declined to hear the case. One of those on the First Circuit panel on the case was Judge Tauro's friend from when their chambers were across the hall in the old courthouse—Sandy Lynch.

> *Sandy Lynch:* We reversed him because in our view the conditions did not exist that would allow him to reopen the case and enter new relief. But we reversed him acknowledging that he had made major contributions in that institutional reform case that needed to be given credit. Joe is a guy very much in touch with the reality of life, and he has a big heart and a lot of sympathy for those who are disfavored in our society.

In the gallery for Tauro's court hearings on closing Fernald, as they had been for so many hearings over the years, were many of the parents, although the one who started it all, Ben Ricci, had died in 2006.

> *Joe Tauro:* I was their hero, but they were the real heroes—the parents and the people who worked there. After a day of being emotionally battered on a facility tour I would get in the car or bus and go home, but the parents of the intellectually disabled have to deal with it every day. It's not going to go away. They go to sleep, and they wake up, and the first thing in the morning they are faced with it again. Their kid is institutionalized.
>
> In the hearing over Romney's plans to close Fernald, they were there again. I know what it's going to be like because every time we have a hearing the courtroom is packed with these people whose faces have gotten a lot older over the last thirty-five years. Mine too, but I think I look like a baby compared to some of them. These are the family members, and this is like a town meeting.

Asked to look back on the long history of these litigations, Tauro invokes a lesson from the ski slopes.

> *Joe Tauro:* I think the break I got was that I didn't look at the whole thing at once. I think if I had any idea at the beginning when I went out there to Belchertown what was going to be facing me, with five institutions and millions and millions of dollars spent, and how many lives were affected, I might have choked on it a little bit.
>
> I remember the first time I went skiing, and a ski instructor took me up, and I thought I was on top of the Alps because I'd never been that high. The instructor said to me: "Always remember, Joe, you're not going to ski the whole thing at once. What you do is you pick a spot— you see that tree down there? We're going to ski to that tree, and then when we get there we're going to pick another spot and we're going to try to go to that. And little by little we chip away at it and then we're down the mountain and we come back up and do it again." I think that's what happened here. I was wise enough not to let the enormity of the thing itself overwhelm me. We just took it a piece at a time.

Michael Dukakis, who was governor for one term early in the litigations and then for another term during the period leading up to the end of court supervision, sees the case as an example of effective judicial activism.

> *Michael Dukakis:* There had been repeated investigations of these institutions going way back, including in the days of Volpe's administration, as I used to remind Joe on occasion that up until the parents brought suit and Joe's involvement as judge, nothing had been done.
>
> I use this as a case study in the leadership course I teach at UCLA and at Northeastern. Joe was political and activist in the best sense. He cared about policy. He knew how to use the press and that helped us get the votes for the appropriations we needed.
>
> It is an interesting issue of public policy as to what extent the federal courts should be involved in matters such as this. Of course, the obvious answer is that if we had done it the courts wouldn't have been in it. Periodically you have

Mike Dukakis with Joe and Liz Tauro's children in the 1970s: Joe Jr., Chris, Beth

COURTESY OF HON. JOSEPH L. TAURO

> particular issues that need the force of the court behind them to get resolved. The Boston Harbor clean-up, which Judge David Mazzone was so instrumental in, is another example.
>
> Once the court gets into something like this it isn't easy, but I'm not sure Joe was there to make it easy. I came in when there was huge unemployment and the biggest deficit proportionally in the country, and I had to raise taxes significantly. We had all kinds of demands on the state budget and everybody was mad at us. But we had a judge who said: "Look, I don't care what your problems are. My job is to make sure that these folks get the rights that I believe they are entitled to and which you have conceded they have. You've got to tax? Tough."
>
> When it was over we had facilities that were the best or among the best in the country. I take some credit for that, Bellotti deserves a lot of credit, and of course the advocates and the parents like Ben Ricci—who was absolutely relentless—deserve huge credit, but Joe was the key.

To Tom Dwyer, who had known Tauro since Tauro's early days in private practice and state government, and later appeared before him a number of times, Tauro's background made him the perfect judge to handle the mental health cases.

> *Tom Dwyer:* Tauro is a guy with a lot of empathy. He didn't develop that sitting on the bench; he got it before that, when he was sitting in his law office in Lynn at six or seven or eight o'clock at night, and people are coming in, telling him about their problems. That's also where he became a scrapper. Not all

Tom Dwyer. Dwyer grew up around the State House, before going on to become a prosecutor and then a leading criminal defense attorney. He also served as President of the Boston Bar Association.

COURTESY OF THOMAS DWYER

of the judges are scrappers, but Joe is. At the same time, his time at the State House made him very sophisticated in the game. He knew how deals were done, and he knew when a ballgame was being prepared. He could see it 100 yards away. I'm not sure that "schemer" is always the perfect word, but you had to be a schemer to succeed in the mental health cases, and Joe could do that. He had seen line items; he knew how they worked.

The great judges are the ones who are known for moving things. This is where people make history. Joe knew how to move power. He moved a giant institution in a huge way.

CHAPTER 16

The Gay Marriage Cases

As Tauro reached and passed the age of seventy, at which his father had faced mandatory retirement under state law, Tauro faced no such restraint under federal law, and he continues to carry a full case load. One of those cases would thrust him back into the national spotlight.

In the spring of 2004, Massachusetts' highest court, the Supreme Judicial Court held, in a 5–2 opinion, that same-sex couples had a right to marry protected by the Massachusetts State Constitution. Opponents of same-sex marriage immediately challenged the decision in federal court, seeking an injunction that would prohibit the Commonwealth from issuing marriage licenses to same-sex couples. Plaintiffs were the Liberty Counsel, the Catholic Action League, eleven state lawmakers, and conservative legal groups in Boston, Michigan, and Mississippi. The case was drawn to Joe Tauro, who heard arguments and then denied the requested relief. Tauro held that the Supreme Judicial Court had "the authority to interpret, and reinterpret, if necessary, the term marriage as it appears in the Massachusetts Constitution."[1] The First Circuit agreed with Tauro, and affirmed.[2]

Five years later, in 2009, the issue of gay marriage was back in Massachusetts federal court, and again Tauro was presiding. This time there were two cases: one brought by seven same-sex couples married in Massachusetts and three same-sex spouses; the second brought by the Commonwealth itself. Both challenged the application of the Federal Defense of Marriage Act (DOMA). Enacted in 1996, DOMA defined marriage for the purpose of federal law as "only a legal union between one man and one woman as husband and wife." Defendants in the case were the United States and various agencies of the federal government. President Obama had advocated the repeal of DOMA, but the administration nevertheless felt obligated to defend the case and did so.

At stake for the individual plaintiffs were federal benefits under a number of federal programs, principally including Social Security, the Federal Employee Health Benefits Program, the Federal Employees Dental and Vision Program, and the right to file a simple federal tax return. At stake for the Commonwealth was the extent of federal support for the state Medicaid program known as MassHealth, and the possible denial of Veterans Administration funding for two state cemeteries for veterans because of the Commonwealth's intention to allow same-sex spouses to be interred there.

Since the facts in the case were largely undisputed, there was no need for a trial. Rather, the federal government moved to dismiss both cases, while the plaintiffs in each case moved for summary judgment. Both parties filed extensive briefs, while the plaintiffs also submitted affidavits detailing the impact of DOMA on various federal programs and also an affidavit on the history of marriage regulation in the United States.

In the spring of 2010, before a packed courtroom, Tauro held two lengthy hearings on the cross-motions. Lawyers and spectators were surprised to see the seventy-eight-year-old judge standing throughout the hearings.

> *Joe Tauro:* I am subject to sciatica, and my physical therapist told me that the worst thing you can do is to sit. He told me to stand as much as possible while I work, so I have been doing that. I have a new desk in my office that I stand at, and I stand very often in court. I think it also helps to keep me alert.

On July 8, 2010, Tauro issued his opinions in the cases, deciding them both in favor of plaintiffs.[3] In the individual plaintiffs' case, he held that DOMA violated plaintiffs' rights to equal protection under the law.

The pivotal question in most equal protection cases is the standard of review employed by the court in evaluating the statute in question. Statutes that adversely impact certain fundamental rights (like free speech) or certain "suspect" classes (like racial minorities that have suffered a history of discrimination) are assessed under a so-called "strict scrutiny" standard, which is almost always the "kiss of death" for the statute. When no fundamental right or suspect class is implicated, the court uses a much more lenient "rational basis" test, whereby a statute is affirmed if it is supported by a rational basis. In the overwhelming majority of rational basis cases, the statute survives review.

Plaintiffs argued that they were entitled to the benefit of a strict scrutiny review both because a fundamental right was involved (their right to maintain the integrity of their existing family relationships), and because as victims of a history of discrimination they should be considered a suspect class. Tauro never reached these arguments. Instead, he held that DOMA failed even the rational basis test. One by one, he rejected the arguments in favor of the statute found in the legislative history: encouraging responsible procreation and child-bearing, defending and nurturing the institution of traditional heterosexual marriage, defending traditional notions of morality, and preserving scarce resources. Then he rejected two separate rationales offered by the Justice Department lawyers in the case: preserving the status quo pending resolution of the debate over same-sex marriage taking place in the states; and making an incremental response to a new social problem. Tauro found each of these purposes either unrelated to the Act, or inherently discriminatory. In the end, he found that "when the proffered rationales for a law are clearly and manifestly implausible, a reviewing court may infer that animus is the only explicable basis."[4] He concluded that "it is only irrational prejudice that motivates the challenged classification."[5]

> *Joe Tauro:* Going with the rational basis review was the key decision I made. I decided not to fiddle around with it; just take it full bore and call it ridiculous. There is no rational basis for it. Even though the rational basis is a hard one to win, here it was so outrageous that you could go that way, and I did.

In the other companion case brought by the Commonwealth, Tauro again ruled for the plaintiff, the Commonwealth. The Equal Protection Clause being inapplicable to the Commonwealth, the opinion instead relied primarily on the Tenth Amendment, holding that the matter of defining marriage was a power that had been, and should remain, for the individual states to decide.

Tauro's gay marriage decisions were greeted with warm praise on the editorial pages of the *New York Times,* the *Boston Globe,* and in other liberal quarters; equally strong condemnation came from most conservatives. There were some on each side, however, who paused to consider the possible implications of Tauro's heavy reliance on the Tenth Amendment in the Commonwealth's suit, given that the Amendment has been a traditional favorite of conservatives and often relied on as a basis for opposing federal laws regarded as overreaching. This led to the possibility that Tauro's decision—should it survive appeal—might later be cited favorably in other contexts by those who have opposed it. Tauro himself was surprised that the decisions didn't elicit more direct criticism:

> *Joe Tauro:* I was told that one guy called the office to say that I was a lousy Catholic, and he called me a few choice names, but that was about it.

In February 2011, the administration announced that it would not be appealing Tauro's decisions in the DOMA case. Rather, in a dramatic reversal of the positions the Department of Justice had argued in the case, Attorney General Eric Holder announced in a letter to Congress that the administration had concluded that classifications based on sexual orientation should be subject to strict scrutiny, and that DOMA was therefore unconstitutional. That was not necessarily the end of the case, however, as the Republican-led House of Representatives then began to debate whether to intervene in the case in order to appeal.

To one of Tauro's former clerks who had been there when the *Rogers* decision was handed down, and when biweekly hearings on Fernald were a staple of the court docket, Tauro's decisions in the Defense of Marriage Act cases fit a pattern.

> *Don Frederico:* The thing that has always impressed me most about Judge Tauro is his commitment to the Constitution and constitutional rights. That was the basis for *Fernald* and for *Rogers,* and it was the basis for the DOMA decisions also. He, more than anyone I have ever known, has a deep abiding commitment to the United States Constitution.

Joe Tauro and his former law clerk Don Frederico. Frederico went on to become President of the Boston Bar Association

COURTESY OF HON. JOSEPH L. TAURO

> He is also very compassionate. The reason you see decisions like those is because he has a lot of compassion for people, and he thinks the law should protect people from suffering at the hands of government.

Writing in *The Atlantic* in the summer of 2011, Andrew Cohen wrote that the Defense of Marriage Act was on the ropes, and he credited Judge Tauro for that:

> We wouldn't be where we are today on the Defense of Marriage Act—the White House backing away from it in court, opponents receding into the background, the Congress on the prowl—if Judge Tauro had not issued that ruling last July. Or if he had authored a ruling that was less unequivocal than the one he issued. For he didn't just strike down the DOMA, he eviscerated it. And in doing so he gave legal and political cover for all that has come since.[6]

NOTES

1 *Largess v. Supreme Judicial Court,* 317 F. Supp. 2d 77, 83 (D. Mass. 2004).

2 *Largess v. Supreme Judicial Court,* 373 F.3d 219 (1st Cir. 2004).

3 *See Gill v. Office of Personnel Mgmt.,* 699 F. Supp. 2d 374 (D. Mass. 2010); *Commonwealth v. U.S. Dep't of Health & Human Servs.,* 698 F. Supp. 2d 234 (D. Mass. 2010).

4 *Gill,* 699 F. Supp. 2d at 396 (quoting *Lofton v. Sec'y of the Dep't of Children & Family Servs.,* 377 F.3d 1275, 1280 (11th Cir. 2004)).

5 *Id.* at 397.

6 Andrew Cohen, *Why the Defense of Marriage Act is on the Ropes,* THE ATLANTIC, July 20, 2011.

CHAPTER 17

The Judge Opines

Defending Lawyers

Joe Tauro has never been afraid of the heat he has taken for sentences that have often been perceived as soft, just as he has not been shy about defending another unpopular cause: lawyers in general, and criminal defense lawyers in particular. Defense of lawyers, and especially of the criminal defense bar, has been a frequent theme of Judge Tauro's speeches over the years. A commencement speech at Suffolk University Law School in 1986 on the theme of "real lawyers" is one example.

> Just about every step of social progress that has been realized in this country was either legislated, adjudicated, or implemented by men and women who serve their communities as "real lawyers." Real lawyers: don't knuckle under in the face of adversity; aren't afraid to represent clients with whom they disagree philosophically; understand and don't shrink from the reality that controversy is a lawyer's stock in trade; believe in the sacred constitutional principle that the accused are presumed innocent, and fight hard to protect that presumption, regardless of what the rest of the world may think of them or their clients.[1]

In a speech to the National Association of Criminal Defense Attorneys two years later, Judge Tauro was back on the same stump:

> Ours is a noble profession. Lawyers make a real difference for the people of this country. Don't ever forget that. And don't let anyone else forget it either.[2]

Judge Tauro is a proud member of the bar who has always defended the legal profession and lauded the contributions lawyers make to a democratic society. There are a few lawyers, now departed, who really stand out in his mind.

> *Joe Tauro:* Earle Cooley is one. He tried four or five cases before me, and he always did a magnificent job. One thing you always knew with Cooley was that there was a part of every case that he considered key. Everything would be going along, and there would be a question asked of the witness. "Objection, your honor," would come out in this loud, booming voice and you knew that this was the franchise point in the trial. "May we approach the bench, your honor?" Then he would always make a very solid argument. I don't think he ever lost a case in my courtroom. He was a brilliant lawyer.
>
> J. Newton Esdaile was another one I admired very much. He was a classmate of my father at B.U. Law. They were good friends. He was a big man who had a majesty about him in a nice way. He was irreverent and funny as hell. He never took himself seriously, but boy was he a killer in court. Even in his later years he would come to court and do some pretrials, and he would lay out the pretrial better than most people would lay out their case at trial.
>
> Another was Richard Egbert, the criminal defense lawyer, who died suddenly at age fifty—a great loss.
>
> We have so many people who have been great lawyers in this court of ours, it's hard to pick a few. What we are talking about are people who you would pay money to get in and watch try a case. These lawyers are so good and so well prepared, and they do such a terrific job. You literally would buy a ticket to go and I'm getting paid to preside. It makes it a privilege, but we don't want to talk about it that way too many times because they'll say we don't need a pay raise—we're getting compensated in other ways.

Judicial Compensation

Judge Tauro's comment about not wanting to talk too much about enjoyment of the job lest it be used against him in the compensation debate is made only partially in jest. Judicial compensation is a sore point for him. During much of the time he has been on the bench, the real value of judges' salaries has declined.

> *Joe Tauro:* The last year I practiced law before I came on the bench I made $196,000. That was in 1971. I took the [court] job at a salary of $40,000—less than a quarter of what I was making in private practice. I knew what I was doing when I took the pay cut, but what I deeply resent is that federal judges have not received the same cost-of-living increases that others have gotten, and our salaries have not kept up with inflation. We are making less in real dollars than we were years ago.

In 1989 Congress finally addressed the issue, passing the Ethics Reform Act, which, among other things, significantly increased the pay of federal judges, while at the same time largely preventing them from earning outside income. To make sure that the old pattern was not repeated, the law also provided, on a going-forward basis, for annual cost-of-living adjustments (COLA) so that the salaries established by the 1989 Act would not be eroded.

When the pay raise legislation was pending, the proposed 50 percent pay raise for judges and Congress drew some negative reaction. Shortly thereafter, the *Boston Globe* carried a story under the headline "Judge Makes Case for Pay Hike."[3] Tauro argued: "One problem the public has with the 50 percent figure was no real appreciation that the pay increase was not a pay raise.... I never dreamed that the $40,000 I got in 1972 would buy only $25,000 worth of food, clothing, and shelter today."[4]

When the pay raise was initially voted down, Judge Tauro was again quoted in the press: "I am not whining. I am not demoralized. I am determined that it is going to be rectified. To hold the judicial branch hostage is an outrage."[5]

The Ethics Reform Act did not work as intended for long. Beginning in 1995, and again in 1996, 1997, and 1999, Congress passed and President Clinton signed statutes that expressly barred the COLAs for federal judges from taking effect. Many judges were furious, and a class action resulted. One of the plaintiffs was Joe Tauro.

> *Joe Tauro:* The lead plaintiff was Spencer Williams, a judge in California, who was the initial leader. He did a great job. I was one of the other leaders. I did a lot of work on the complaint,

> which we vetted among a lot of judges around the country to make sure it was very strong, and it really was.

The plaintiff judges relied on a clause in the Constitution which provided that "Judges...shall, at stated times, receive for their services, a compensation, which shall not be diminished during their continuance in office." The judges' position was that removing a statutory entitlement to a COLA was a diminution of their pay, which violated the Constitution. The government argued that Congress had the authority over judicial pay; it had authorized the COLA adjustment by statute, and it could take it away the same way, as long as it did so before the COLA took effect.

The judges prevailed in the trial court, but on appeal the Federal Circuit voted 2–1 to reverse. A petition asking the entire federal court to hear the case en banc failed, despite some passionate dissenting opinions.

At that point, the plaintiff judges faced the question of whether to seek review from the U.S. Supreme Court.

> *Joe Tauro:* The question was whether or not we had enough votes there. We were confident that we had four votes for certiorari, but it wasn't clear whether we could get five votes to win the case, given that some judges felt it was unholy to sue over pay. In the end we decided not to go for certiorari because our lawyers were afraid we might lose the case and that would make things harder in the future.

The case left a bad taste in Judge Tauro's mouth.

> *Bill Young:* Joe was angry at the judges of the Federal Circuit, and he was angry at Judge Posner out of Chicago, who was extremely wealthy and had spoken out against the pay raise. I had a retired Massachusetts state judge here to lunch one day and we sat with Joe. Somewhere along the way the judge made a pro-Posner comment and Joe was not pleased and told him so. It was an awkward lunch.

In the wake of the Federal Circuit's ruling, judicial pay continued to languish. In his year-end report in 2006, U.S. Supreme Court Chief Justice John Roberts took on the issue forcefully, making it the only subject of his report to emphasize that the situation had reached what he felt was a "Constitutional crisis." He noted that since 1969 the pay of federal judges, adjusted for inflation, had dropped 23.9 percent. During that period judges had gone from making over 40 percent more than senior law professors to making only about half of what those professors make. The number of judges leaving the profession was on the rise.

Roberts' speech did not have the intended effect on Congress, but the judges are not sitting still. Another case has been filed. Tauro is not a plaintiff this time, but that doesn't mean he isn't passionate on the subject.

> *Joe Tauro:* I am not actively involved this time, but I am very supportive of it. The theory of this case is that the earlier case was wrongly decided. This time they are looking to take the case to the Supreme Court because it's a different court now. There are about ten different years when Congress hasn't given us the COLA adjustments, and when you add those up and compound them, it amounts to big dollars. It's going to be a big case, and we think we are going to win.

It Takes a Team

Another subject that Tauro is passionate about is his staff. He is a popular boss who treats those who work with him with respect and warmth, and he is quick to share the credit. For most of his time on the bench, he has drawn his law clerks exclusively from his *alma maters,* Brown University and Cornell Law School, and from the school where he taught and which his father attended, Boston University School of Law.

Tauro has strong feelings about all three schools, and he has been impressed.

> *Joe Tauro:* When I interview law clerk applicants, I make a couple of points very clear. I tell them that the clerkship is not merely a fourth year of law school, or just another research assignment. It will be their first year of true professional responsibility where they play a vital role in the administration of justice. I tell them that they are the very foundation of everything I will do. Their research gives me the parameters and options of what actions I may and should take

2010 Staff Christmas party. First Row: Zita Lovett, courtroom clerk; Judge Tauro; Dale Berthiaume, judicial assistant; Barbara Sakurai, retired court reporter; Mary (Chickie) Coughlin Cummings, retired courtoom clerk. Second Row: Michael (Mickey) Klebanov, law clerk 2010–2011; Zsaleh E. Harivandi, law clerk 2010-2011; Carol Scott, court reporter.

COURTESY OF HON. JOSEPH L. TAURO

in the variety of complex issues that are a federal judge's daily stock in trade. And I let them know that I will depend on them to make sure that the menu of opportunity they lay out for me is full and complete.

My law clerks have been uniformly excellent. Their research and writing skills are superb. And, most important of all, has been their loyalty and their dedication to excellence. I am proud to have each and every one of my law clerks as my close and cherished friend. (A list of Judge Tauro's law clerks, with their dates of service, is included in this book's appendix.)

John Nadas: I remember during the first week of my clerkship a criminal case I was assigned to went to trial. As the law clerk on a case, you were always in court for any courtroom activity on that case. At one point a cross-examination was completed, the examining lawyer sat down, and opposing counsel started to get up. The judge said: "Wait a minute. We are going to take a break. John: Get up here." So I went to side bar. I was scared

> to death, trying to figure out what I had done wrong. He told me there was an important point of cross examination that I should take from what had just happened. The examining lawyer had asked one question too many, and by doing so, he had diluted his point. He had the point, and then he weakened it. The judge told me I should never do that. And that is the way the clerkship went—it was a true apprenticeship. I learned a tremendous amount from the judge about the craft of litigation. He was always teaching us. He was also like a father figure to me. I had a strong father, and he was like another one. He cared a great deal about his clerks as people and he took a great interest in our lives. That has a lot to do with why his clerks and former clerks are such a strong clerk community and also why there is such a feeling of family about his whole courthouse team.

Six courtroom deputies have served under Tauro: Austin Jones, Walter Doherty, Judy Dinneen, Dennis Duggan, Mary Cummings, and Zita Lovett. Again, Tauro waxes warmly about their service:

> *Joe Tauro:* The session simply couldn't run without the dedication and skillful oversight of the courtroom deputies. As the saying goes, they are what make the trains run on time. They create the schedules and, somehow, make it work. It is a high-pressure job, but they meet the challenges with a sure hand and a sense of humor. I am grateful for their dedication and loyalty, and I cherish their friendship.

Tauro also sings the praises of the four court reporters who have worked for him: Bill Curry, Carol Scott, Barbara Sakurai, and Alan Mezzetti.

> *Joe Tauro:* My court reporters have been the most patient and supportive members of the team. Imagine the dedication it takes to listen to every word spoken in the courtroom. They are all real pals.

Finally, there is Judge Tauro's Judicial Assistant, Dale Berthiaume, who has been with him throughout Tauro's thirty-eight years on the bench.

> *Joe Tauro:* Dale is a one-person category. She has been my judicial assistant and loyal friend for the entire time I have been on the bench. I may be replaceable, but she isn't. I love you, Dale.

NOTES

1 *See Judge Tauro Muses on Constitution,* Freedom, DAILY EVENING ITEM (Lynn, Mass.), Mar. 30, 1988.

2 *See Judge Charges Lawyers with Call to Law's High Purpose,* DAILY EVENING ITEM (Lynn, Mass.), Aug. 19, 1988, at 9.

3 Mary Dickman, *Judge Makes Case for Pay Hike,* BOS. GLOBE.

4 *See* Bill McAlister, *The Judiciary's 'Quiet Crisis': Prestige Doesn't Pay the Tuition,* WASH. POST, Jan. 21, 1987, at A19.

5 Alexandre Varney, *Defeat of Raise Blamed on Misunderstanding,* 17 M.L.W. 1023, at 3 (Feb. 13, 1989).

CHAPTER 18

Thoughts on Retirement

A conversation with Joe Tauro about retirement is likely to be brief. He has never been the retiring sort, in any sense of the word. His father had to step down from the Supreme Judicial Court at age seventy under Massachusetts' compulsory retirement rules, and for the rest of his life he missed his work as a judge tremendously. There is no mandatory retirement for federal judges, and Joe Tauro is glad of that. He is seventy-nine, still carrying a full case load, moving it briskly and effectively, and enjoying his job. Should there ever come a point when he loses his effectiveness and hangs on too long, there is a plan in place to deal with that.

> *Joe Tauro:* I have no desire to retire. I enjoy what I do, and I think I'm still good at it. But I've got people who are sworn to tell me when they think I'm not good at it. Mike Mone is one and Michael Ponsor and Howard Pearl are two others. Sometimes you get so in love with the job and your problem is so great you can't even think. You don't believe anybody. These are people I have talked to, letting them know that I want them to tell me if the time ever comes.

> *Michael Ponsor:* If I absolutely had to, I probably would, but I don't think it's ever going to happen, and it would be a chore that I would resist with all my might. I'd be in tears before I even started talking. But I don't think it's going to happen.

> *Mike Mone:* I've said to other people who have become judges: "You've got to have someone who you really trust who can

> come to you and tell you that maybe a lot of people are saying that you're getting too cranky, or whatever it is." Neither Ponsor nor I want to do that in this case. I'd be perfectly happy for Ponsor to do it. This is Alfonse and Gaston. But I think Judge Tauro continues to do a good job.

In the meantime, as the years continue to mount, one person who has had an eye on Judge Tauro's career throughout is the man who nominated him: former Senator Ed Brooke.

> *Ed Brooke:* I remember saying to Joe when I appointed him that I would like for when a plaintiff or a defendant comes into your courtroom that he has the feeling of safety and that he is confident that justice will be done. I think he's done that. He's had some tough cases, and he's handled them with aplomb. I've been very proud of him.
>
> And he is forever grateful. Every year on the anniversary of the day he was sworn in as a judge he calls me and thanks me for the appointment. He tells me that he loves his job, that's it's been a wonderful opportunity, and that he's enjoyed every minute of it. He does this every year, right on the date, and he never misses. Isn't that something? I think the Commonwealth and the people who have come into his court have been the beneficiaries of that appointment.

Another who has followed Tauro's career closely, even as their paths have intersected repeatedly, is his old friend Steve Breyer. His tribute to Judge Tauro on

Joe Tauro and Howard Pearl, May 2008. Pearl became a partner in the Chicago firm of Winston and Strawn.

COURTESY OF HON. JOSEPH L. TAURO

Joe Tauro and Ed Brooke

COURTESY OF HON. JOSEPH L. TAURO

the occasion of Tauro's portrait presentation ended on a poignant note:

Stephen Breyer: In the future, when people say "Tauro, the great judge, the great chief," Massachusetts citizens will ask, "Do you mean Tauro of the state courts or Tauro of the federal courts?" His father would be so proud. So are we all.

APPENDIX

Tauro Law Clerks

Mark Brodin, '72 – '74

Steven Baumohl, '73

Peter Bogle, '73 – '74

Mark Nozette, '74 – '76

James McGuire, '74 – '75

Michael Ponsor, '75 – '76

Ellen Gesmer, '76 – '77

John Nadas, '76 – '77

Marion Bachrach, '77 – '78

Paul Summit, '77 – '78

Roderick MacLeish, '78 – '79

Steven Horowitz, '78 – '79

Mitchell Kaplan, '78 – '79

Thomas Balliett, '79 – '80

Donald Frederico, '79 – '80

John Sander, '80 – '81

Howard Pearl, '80 – '82

Julie Edmond, '81 – '82

Steven Kolyer, '81 – '82

Steven Rosenblum, '82 – '83

Jonathan Chiel, '82 – '83

Margaret Samson, '83 – '84

Robert Manfred, Jr., '83 – '84

Leo Arnaboldi, '84 – '85

Richard Brunell, '84 – '85

Jeffrey Michaelson, '85 – '86

Geoffrey Oliver, '85 – '86

John Kassel, '86 – '87

Benjamin Marcus, '86 – '87

Jane Gallagher, '87 – '88

Frederick Brodie, '87 – '88

Jamin Dershowitz, '88 – '89

Harry Davis, '88 – '89

John Moustakas, '89 – '90

Kenneth Doroshow, '89 – '90

Richard Batchelder, '90 – '91

Seth Farber, '90 – '91

Pamela Moreau, '91 – '92

John Hecht, '91 – '92

Audrey Mark, '92 – '93

Matthew Rita, '92 – '93

Kristopher Brown, '92 – '93

Kimberly Hult, '93 – '94

Peter Schwartz, '93 – '94

Stephen Smerek, '93 – '94

David Stone, '94 – '95

Michael D'Orsi, '94 – '95

Roberto Finzi, '94 – '95

Jeffrey Blum, '95 – '96

J. Richard Doidge, '95 – '96

Gregory Horangic, '95 – '96

Matthew Connolly, '96 – '97

Eric Delinsky, '96 – '97

R. Peter Nessen, '96 – '97

Alexandra Glazier, '97 – '98

John Bueker, '97 – '98

Candace Kronholm, '97 – '98

David Grable, '98 – '99

Michael Dion, '98 – '99

Katherine Ma, '98 – '99

L. Jay Law, '99 – '00

Jonathan Oblak, '99 – '00

Jeff Katz, '00 – '01

Gayle Littleton, '00 – '01

Jason Jones, '01 – '02

Elizabeth Mone, '01 – '02

Caroline Hayday, '02 – '03

Jonathan Francis, '02 – '03

Heather R. Zuzenak, '03 – '04

Christopher B. Harwood, '03 – '04

Christopher P. Coval, '04 – '05

Scott P. Bridge, '04 – '05

Brad S. Weinstein, 8/29 – 11/14/05

Robert W. Sparkes III,
12/12/05 – 9/1/06

Pamela Sawhney, '05 – '06

Stephen F. Rickard, '06 – '07

Peter D. Sax, '06 – '07

Timothy Webster, '07 – '08

Jason B. Frasco, '07 – '08

Kyle R. Taylor, '08 – '09

Jason J. Englund, '08 – '09

Elizabeth (Lizzie) R. Carr, '09 – '10

Susan (Susie) A. Hensler, '09 – '10

Michael Klebanov, '10 – '11

Zsaleh Harivandi, '10 – '11

Ron Ghatan, '11 – '12

Megan (Meg) Larkin, '11 – '12

INDEX

Persons Referenced